DAVID TORRANCE is a [...] ist and broadcaster who specialises in the politics and [...] long-running debate about Scottish indep[...] ducated in Edinburgh, Aberdeen an[...] er a[...] television reporter [...] e i[...] politics at Westminster. For the past [...] a freelance commentator as well as the auth[...] ore than a dozen books about Scottish and [...] iography and history. Like all good Scotsmen he has li[...] London for long stretches, and is currently based there.

Luath Press is an independently owned and managed book publishing company based in Scotland and is not aligned to any political party or grouping.

By the same author

The Scottish Secretaries (Birlinn, 2006)

George Younger: A Life Well Lived (Birlinn, 2008)

'We in Scotland': Thatcherism in a Cold Climate
(Birlinn, 2009)

Noel Skelton and the Property-Owning Democracy
(Biteback, 2010)

*Inside Edinburgh: Discovering the Classic Interiors of
Edinburgh* (Birlinn, 2010) (with Steve Richmond)

Salmond: Against the Odds (Birlinn, 2010, 2011 and 2015)

Great Scottish Speeches I (ed.) (Luath Press, 2011)

David Steel: Rising Hope to Elder Statesman (Biteback, 2012)

Whatever Happened to Tory Scotland? (ed.)
(Edinburgh University Press, 2012)

*The Battle for Britain: Scotland and the Independence
Referendum* (Biteback, 2013)

Great Scottish Speeches II (ed.) (Luath Press, 2013)

*Britain Rebooted: Why Federalism Would be Good for the
Nations and Regions of the UK* (Luath Press, 2014 and 2015)

Scotland's Referendum: A Guide for Voters (Luath Press, 2014)
(with Jamie Maxwell)

*100 Days of Hope and Fear: How Scotland's Referendum was
Lost and Won* (Luath Press, 2014)

Nicola Sturgeon: A Political Life (Birlinn, 2015)

GENERAL ELECTION 2015

A Guide
for Voters

IN SCOTLAND

DAVID TORRANCE

Luath Press Limited
EDINBURGH
www.luath.co.uk

First published 2015

ISBN: 978-1-910745-06-9

The paper used in this book is recyclable.
It is made from low chlorine pulps
produced in a low energy, low emissions
manner from renewable forests.

Printed and bound by
Bell & Bain Ltd., Glasgow

Designed by Tom Bee

Typeset in 10.5 point Din
by 3btype.com

Contents

Foreword by Kevin McKenna

How Westminster Works

1   **Introduction**

2   **Scottish Conservatives**

3   **Scottish Greens**

4   **Scottish Labour Party**

5   **Scottish Liberal Democrats**

6   **Scottish National Party**

7   **UK Independence Party**

8   **Other Parties**

9   **Possible Outcomes**

10   **Constitutional Implications**

Policy Grid

Timeline

Foreword
by Kevin McKenna

I first encountered David Torrance in Inverness at a Scottish National Party conference in 2012 and was keen to tell him how much I had enjoyed his books on Margaret Thatcher and Alex Salmond. Owing to the Scots' unfortunate habit of conferring labels on others I had him down as a Tory, albeit of the progressive and hipster wing (In Scotland you are a Tory if, on meeting a soul for the first time, you haven't abjured 'Thatcher' within the opening minute of a conversation about politics). Perhaps he is, although in his elegant columns for *The Herald* it is pleasingly difficult to detect any solid party allegiance. And although I assume he voted No in the Scottish independence referendum I will never quite be sure.

Thereafter we found ourselves sharing television studios together during the long lead-in to last September 18 where I was struck by an idiosyncratic deployment of his wardrobe as well as a mastery of the nuances of each side's economic and social policies. This made him a thorn in the side of both the Yes and the No camps because there is nothing a professional politician enjoys less than being confronted with someone who has a grasp of the detail as well as the vision.

By then, I was moving towards a Yes vote in the referendum but I remained admiring of David's ability to shine a torch on those big empty spaces where the Yes campaign's proposed fiscal arrangements in an independent Scotland were supposed to reside. Often, on discovering that David was to be my fellow guest on a late-night political slot, I found myself frantically firing up my iPad for the purposes of some last-minute cramming lest my threadbare grasp of detail on some issues be exposed by his cold bullshit-detector.

FOREWORD BY KEVIN McKENNA

And although I was eventually persuaded by the Yes case for independence, albeit with a few misgivings and fuelled a little by a 'what the hell?' approach, I appreciated David's unerring propensity to get up the noses of some nationalists with his *Herald* columns. (Among some of my Nationalist chums you are a vile, Unionist cur if, on first encountering them, you haven't used the word 'Freedom' in the first minute of conversation). That Alex Salmond, who has made getting up the noses of Unionists his lifetime work, was moved to write to *The Herald* to rebuke David ought to be a feather in his cap. 'He doesn't know me at all,' harrumphed our former First Minister, which is palpably not the case if you ever read *Salmond: Against the Odds*.

I am glad David has written this book. On receiving the proofs I immediately put them to good use as research for that week's column in *The Observer*. It will prove to be a boon for every journalist and researcher in Scotland including those who, like me, write about politics from time to time as opposed to being a bona fide political writer. I expect though, that it will prove to be equally invaluable to the voting public at large. Personally, I found the Greens' radical and adventurous policy on future banking arrangements, as set out in these pages, particularly eye-catching.

Scotland's voters are far more knowledgeable about politics and much more sophisticated in the way they use their votes than any previous generation in the democratic age. One of the joys of the referendum campaign was watching people I had known for a long time become utterly engaged with issues which affected their lives but in which they had previously taken only a passing interest.

In this book David sets out concisely, lucidly and without any hint of prejudice, the policies of each of the UK's main political parties as we head towards the Westminster election in May 2015. In doing so he places each of their positions on the compelling issues in the context of their recent journey to where we are now. In the last two chapters he guides us through the maze of options available for every possible outcome on May 7 and how this may affect the country's governance for the next five years (and no, Jim, the party with the biggest number of seats doesn't automatically get to govern). The constitutional ramifications for the UK and for Scotland in particular if the SNP adroitly hold the balance of power, as dealt with here, are profound and far-reaching. These are dealt with in an important closing chapter which acts as a user's manual to understanding each of the constitutional outcomes following an inconclusive result on May 7, though I feel that a second independence referendum may be closer than he thinks.

Every election, of course, is special and produces its own land-mark themes and controversies. But each generation produces a watershed election, one whose outcome has the potential to alter dramatically the course and dynamics of the country for 15 years or so and thus come to define an era. Harold Wilson's victory in 1964 was one such as was Margaret Thatcher's in 1979 and Tony Blair's in 1997. The 2015 Westminster election, I think, is of that ilk. It occurs following a febrile eight-month period in which the SNP, despite seeing their independence dream vanquished (for a while, at least) have driven right up to the doors of Westminster and parked their tanks on College Green.

FOREWORD BY KEVIN McKENNA

We will know soon enough if the massive surge in support for the SNP predicted by all the opinion polls from October to March translates into their annexing of Scotland after May 7. If that happens, then deal or no deal with the party of government, Britain will be set fair for unknown waters. This book should be the voters' companion in choosing the route and in helping us to keep track of the horse-trading which will occur thereafter.

Kevin McKenna
March 2015

How Westminster Works

Since the 1707 Treaty of Union that formed 'Great Britain' in place of Scotland and England, both have been represented – along with Wales and (Northern) Ireland – at the Westminster Parliament in London. Then as now Parliament meets at the invitation of the monarch, who is the hereditary and therefore unelected head of state. Originally Scotland had just 45 MPs though this was later increased to 72. Under the terms of the 1998 Scotland Act, however, this was reduced to 59 prior to the 2005 general election. Elections to the House of Commons now take place every five years.

Each MP represents a territorial 'constituency' in the House of Commons, which is elected under a system called first-past-the-post. And although the Scottish Parliament now controls most domestic policy (see below), the UK government – comprising MPs and Members of the House of Lords – still deals with 'reserved' matters such as foreign affairs, defence, the economy, monetary policy, broadcasting, energy, inter-national development and welfare. Representing Scotland in this respect is a Secretary of State for Scotland, who sits in the Cabinet, and a small department called the Scotland Office (from 1885 until 1999 this was called the Scottish Office, and had much more power than at present). Among the House of Commons' Select Committees is one covering Scottish Affairs, which scrutinises the UK government's functions in relation to Scotland.

At the 2010 general election the Labour Party won 41 Scottish constituencies, the Liberal Democrats 11, the SNP 6 and the Conservatives just one. The SNP often points out that under what it refers to as the 'Westminster system' Scotland can often end up being governed by a UK administration that a majority of Scottish voters did not vote for – i.e. during the period of Conservative government from 1979 to 1997 when no more than 22 Tory MPs (and after 1987 half that number) were returned in Scotland. Of course this can go the other way, so between 1997 and 2010 Labour had a majority of MPs in both Scotland and the UK as a whole.

Scotland is also represented in the Upper House of the UK Parliament, the House of Lords. Until 1999 this comprised a mix of hereditary (inherited) and 'life' (appointed) peers, but at that point all but 92 hereditaries were expelled, meaning the current House of Lords is predominantly appointed. There are currently around 800 members, many of whom are Scottish, although it is difficult to say exactly how many because they do not represent geographical constituencies. The House of Lords scrutinises legislation approved by the House of Commons (the Lower House) and can amend Bills, although it is not allowed to prevent them becoming law. Until 2009 the Upper House also acted as the highest court of appeal in the UK (though not for Scottish criminal cases), a function now fulfilled by a Supreme Court also situated in Westminster. Of its 12 'Justices', two are generally specialists in Scots Law.

Introduction 1

Democratic elections are, by their very nature, important events: in a democracy an electorate chooses its government via a secret ballot, and the resulting administration can go on to exercise its mandate in several ways. But some elections are more important than others, and there is a general consensus that the UK general election due on 7 May 2015 is such an election.

Even veteran pundits and pollsters are unsure as to the most likely outcome, although most are agreed it may produce another 'hung' or 'balanced' Parliament, i.e. one in which no single party has an overall majority. Although that also happened at the last UK general election five years ago such an outcome is still a relative rarity under an electoral system (known as first-past-the-post) that generally produces majority governments.

One has to reach back to February 1974 to find a similar scenario, while before that 1910 (another year, like 1974, in which two elections were held) stands out as having produced a Parliament in which the two largest parties (at that time the Liberals and Conservatives) were roughly even in terms of seats. But while history is useful for context, it only takes us so far in 2015: each election takes place, of course, in a unique context of events, personalities and debate.

So uncertainty plays its part in making the forthcoming general election an interesting one, but – unusually for a UK ballot – it also has a strongly Scottish dimension. Since the end of 2014 there has been a growing recognition that the Scottish National Party (SNP) is likely to do well (certainly judging by polls) and therefore hold a position of some influence should a 'hung' Parliament come to pass.

1

It means that instead of the SNP only wielding power via the devolved Scottish Parliament in Edinburgh it could end up exercising power at Westminster too. This could take many forms, most likely an informal arrangement with the Labour Party (Nicola Sturgeon, the SNP leader, has ruled out any support for the Conservatives). Even if neither scenario transpires, it seems likely the SNP will have a greater presence in the House of Commons than ever before.

All this, of course, is conjecture, predictions based on the available evidence, but general elections can also be unpredictable things. In 1992, for example, it was widely expected Labour would form a government (it did not), while five years later, when Labour did win, most political observers were surprised at how large its majority was (a staggering 179 seats more than the combined total of every other party in parliament). The weeks immediately before an election are chock full of analysis, speculation and polling all contrived to figure out what is likely to happen. Often it is completely wrong.

But then Scottish and UK politics, particularly since devolution in the late 1990s, have become increasingly complex. Rather than one set of elections to a single UK-wide Parliament, there are now separate ballots for the Scottish Parliament in Edinburgh, the National Assembly for Wales in Cardiff, the Northern Ireland Assembly in Belfast and a Mayor and Assembly in London. Add to that a myriad of local government elections; five-yearly elections to the European Parliament in Brussels (and Strasbourg) and occasional referendums (most notably that on Scottish independence last year), and, at times, it can be difficult to keep up.

Thus the publication of this *Guide for Voters*, a sort of sequel to a similarly short book produced a few months before the independence referendum on 18 September 2014 (co-written by myself and the journalist Jamie Maxwell). That was intended to summarise the main points of debate in a lengthy and often complex debate, cutting through claim and counter-claim and hopefully making it a little bit easier for readers to decide whether to vote Yes or No to independence.

So what follows is, at first, a concise guide to what each of the major political parties contesting this general election are offering both in UK and Scottish terms. The chapters are in alphabetical order to avoid accusations of bias, while the text in each case includes minimal analysis. It should also be noted that as this book went to print before the publication of any party manifestos, it is thus only a general guide. Each party, however, co-operated with its production, and thus the reader can be confident that each chapter is an accurate summary of each party's agenda. In addition, each chapter includes a speech by the relevant party leader outlining their thinking on key issues in his or her own words.

Since 1999 political parties in Scotland have faced a problem when it comes to campaigning in UK general elections, for they often end up discussing policy pledges or issues that are already devolved to the Scottish Parliament in Edinburgh. All parties have been guilty of this, but in the text that follows I do my best to make the distinction clear. Given that Holyrood elections are due to take place in May 2016 it is obviously tempting for politicians to campaign with both ballots in mind.

A couple of concluding chapters will then consider possible outcomes once all the votes have been counted after polls close at 10pm on 7 May. The result should become clear early the following morning but, as outlined above, is likely to be highly unpredictable. The UK, of course, does not have a written constitution, but in Chapter 9 I do my best to guide the reader through the likely course of constitutional events, based on precedent and the *Cabinet Manual*, published in 2010. The final chapter considers possible implications once (and if) a new government is formed, i.e. further devolution to Scotland, the introduction of English Votes for English Laws, a possible referendum on the UK's relationship with the European Union, and so on.

There are some things this *Guide for Voters* cannot hope to predict, for example the prospect of what is known as 'tactical' voting, or indeed turnout. It is not yet clear if the unprecedented degree of voter engagement experienced on 18 September 2014 – an 85 per cent turnout – will be sustained on 7 May 2015. Turnout in Scotland at the last general election was nearly 64 per cent, while at the last Holyrood elections in May 2011 it was just 50 per cent, so there is at least the prospect of an increase. Finally, one feature of this general election has been known for quite some time, i.e. the date. Under Section 1 of the Fixed-term Parliaments Act of 2011, polling is due to occur on the first Thursday in May of the fifth year after the previous general election. Whether that remains the case following this election is, however, a moot point.

David Torrance
March 2015
@davidtorrance

www.davidtorrance.com

Scottish Conservatives

Since the 1980s UK general elections have found the Scottish Conservative and Unionist Party (SCUP) in an unusual position. Across the UK the Conservative Party (of which the SCUP forms part) was either the main opposition party or in government, either with an overall majority (in 1983, 1987, 1992) or as the lead partner in a coalition (2010). In Scotland, however, it won just ten (out of 73) seats in 1987, 11 in 1992, none in 1997, and only one seat (out of 59 from 2005 onwards) in 2001, 2005 and 2010.

Although under the 'rules of the game' this disparity between the party's performance in Scotland and the rest of Great Britain (the Conservatives have little presence in Northern Ireland) did not interfere with its political ability to form UK governments, it did give rise to increasing problems of legitimacy in Scotland. The establishment of a Scottish Parliament in 1999 was intended to neutralise this perceived lack of 'mandate', but it never quite went away.

It was all a far cry from the Conservative Party's status in Scotland in the pre- and post-war era. Between 1912 and 1965 there existed a separate organisation called the 'Scottish Unionist Party', which was affiliated to the UK Conservative Party and did rather well, even winning a majority of votes and seats (albeit in an electoral alliance with a smaller Unionist party) in Scotland at the 1955 general election. It did so by playing the 'Scottish card' (much as the SNP do today), advocating what it called 'Scottish Control of Scottish Affairs', although it preferred administrative rather legislative devolution.

Between the late 1970s and 1997, however, the Scottish Conservatives resolutely opposed devolution for Scotland, and

2

even after 1999 often gave the impression that it accepted the new constitutional status quo only grudgingly. More recently, under the leadership of Ruth Davidson, the party has attempted to position itself ahead of the constitutional curve by advocating greater devolution, first with its own Strathclyde Commission and, following the independence referendum, as part of the cross-party Smith Commission. Its website describes the Scottish Conservatives as 'a patriotic party of the Scottish centre-right which stands for freedom, enterprise, community and equality of opportunity'.

Below are details of the Scottish Conservative Party's pledges when it comes to further devolution, but at the UK level it argues that the forthcoming election is 'one of the most important' in recent history, a choice between another Conservative government that will 'keep us on track', providing 'security for families, businesses and the country', or the 'chaos' of a 'weak Ed Miliband government propped up by an SNP which is still trying to wreck the United Kingdom'. It claims only the Conservatives can 'stand up to the SNP and keep Ed Miliband out of Downing Street'.

Since entering government in 2010 the Conservatives say they have been 'working hard' on a 'long-term economic plan to turn Britain around', halving the UK's deficit, reducing income tax for 25 million people, capping benefits 'to reward work', putting 1.85 million people back in employment and increasing the state pension by £800. It also takes credit for having 'led the campaign to keep Scotland in the UK'.

Although the party regards all of the above as 'a good start' it says 'the job is far from finished – there is much more we still have to do', thus another five years of Conservative government is needed to 'finish the job' and ensure that:

- Hard-working families have the reward of a meaningful job and a decent standard of living, because their taxes are low and our debts are being paid off; encourage enterprise and back small business, keeping jobs taxes low and cutting red tape.

- People have the security of owning their own home and the financial independence to enjoy retirement.

- Run a surplus so that we start paying down our debts and keep our economy secure, crack down on tax avoidance and ensure those who can afford to pay the most do.

- Continue to increase spending on the NHS so everyone gets the care they need; deliver tax-free childcare and a tax cut for married couples – to help families get on in life.

- Cut income tax for 30 million people and take everyone who earns less than £12,500 out of income tax altogether, back aspiration by raising the 40p tax threshold – so that no one earning less than £50,000 pays it.

- Reward those who have worked hard by continuing to increase the Basic State Pension through the triple lock, reward saving by introducing a new single-tier pension and give people the freedom to invest and spend their pension as they like and pass it on to loved ones tax-free.

2

- Conduct a UK-wide referendum by the end of 2017 on whether the UK should remain in the European Union.

When it comes to Scotland, the Conservatives say an election win would mean Scotland remaining 'a proud member of the United Kingdom, with its currency and economy secured as a result', while it would act quickly to legislate for the devolution of more power to Holyrood based on the recommendations of the cross-party Smith Commission, with a Scotland Bill included in the first Queen's Speech after the election. (Legislation would also be introduced to give effect to 'English Votes for English Laws', under which Scottish MPs' right to vote on 'England-only' measures would be restricted.) Building a 'strong Scotland in a strong United Kingdom' would, says the party, enable it to:

- **REDUCE THE DEFICIT to deal with our debts, safeguard our economy for the long term and keep mortgage rates low.**

- **CUT INCOME TAX and freeze fuel duty to help hardworking people be more financially secure.**

- **CREATE MORE JOBS by backing small business and enterprise with better infrastructure and lower jobs taxes.**

- **CAP WELFARE and work to control immigration so our economy delivers for people who want to work hard and play by the rules.**

- **IMPROVE OUR SCHOOLS so every child gets the best chance in life no matter their background.**

In terms of specific Scottish policies (many of which are devolved), meanwhile, it would like the Scottish Government to:

- Examine the entire basket of future devolved taxes as well as public spending through the 'Commission for Competitive and Fair Taxation in Scotland'; introduce incentives to help small businesses pay the living wage.

- Introduce 'childcare credits' to offer maximum flexibility to parents who want to use their statutory childcare entitlement; repeal named person provisions in the Children and Young People Act; pursue a wide education reform agenda in Scotland based on school diversity, school autonomy and parental choice.

- Protect revenue and capital NHS spending in real terms; hire an additional 1,000 nurses by reintroducing prescription charges; pilot a network of recovery centres to relieve pressure on A&E departments.

- Conduct a review of Police Scotland to address issues with accountability to Parliament as well as local communities; introduce real work schemes in prisons to offer meaningful rehabilitation within the prison estate; legislate for tougher community sentences and stronger punishment for breaches; introduce whole life orders in Scotland.

- Reform the planning system to give more power to local communities; improve community transport by extending the New Computerised Transit System (NCTS) to community transport providers and aligning with the Scottish Planning Assessment.

- Extend the provision of affordable housing through incentives and broader grant support; accelerate the current superfast broadband rollout and commit to rolling out broadband to all rural premises.

For more information, please see
www.scottishconservatives.com

David Cameron MP, speech to the Scottish Conservative Party Conference, 20 February 2015

Now the [referendum] campaign is over, the question is settled, but friends – a major risk to Scotland's future remains. [Ed] Miliband and [Ed] Balls. We fought to stop the risk of break-up. Now we've got to fight the risk of bankruptcy. Seventy-six days from now there is an election. And the choice could not be more clear. On one side of the choice, there's us – the Conservatives. A strong team with a long-term economic plan that is delivering for Scotland.

And I tell everyone in this hall, with just 76 days to go – get out there and tell people what we've done. Tell them what we found, what we've delivered – and why. We found the scandal of a pensions system that punished savers, that left elderly people counting the pennies and worried about the future. So we ended the hated means test, we brought in a record rise in the State Pension.

And why? Because Conservatives believe that if you have worked hard your whole life – you deserve dignity and security in old age. We found a tax system that slammed businesses and hammered low earners, so we cut taxes, making sure no-one pays a penny in income tax on the first £10,000 they earn, giving a tax cut to 2.3 million Scots.

Why? Because we're Conservatives – we get that it's your money, not Government's, and we should never take a penny more than we have to. We came in and found the misery of mass unemployment. So we reformed welfare to make work pay, backed business, invested in Scotland, created 187,000 jobs here in Scotland.

Why does this matter so much? Because we know that work is the best route to security and building yourself a better life, that a job isn't just good for your bank account but good for your self-esteem and good for your soul. Unemployment down, investment up last year – the fastest-growing major economy in the world.

And friends – if there's one thing I want you to remember on the doorstep, it's this. If anyone says 'what have the Tories ever done for Scotland?' – tell them this. We've seen over 100 new jobs created each and every day in Scotland since this Government's been in office, over 100 people with more hope and more security and that is a record to be truly proud of.

That's just one side of the choice. On the other side: Ed Miliband in Downing Street. And if you thought the ultimate nightmare scenario was a Labour Government? Try this: Labour and the SNP in Government – a unique, unprecedented coalition of the people who would break up our country and the people who would bankrupt our country.

The only people who can stop them are us – the Party in this room. So let us be clear to the people of Scotland. A vote for anyone other than the Conservatives risks Ed Miliband becoming Prime Minister, leading an unstable minority Government. A vote for the SNP is a vote for Labour in Government. Nicola Sturgeon has made clear she is up for a coalition with Ed Miliband. As Ruth [Davidson] has put it, the SNP and Labour are halfway up the aisle together already.

She's right. They've picked out the wedding list. They've booked the honeymoon – probably to North Korea. They've set up a joint account – unlimited overdraft obviously. And so if you vote for anyone else apart from the Conservatives, you are voting for this outcome.

Labour in Government. Ed Miliband in Downing Street and the very real prospect of Alex Salmond coming in through the back door. Like a horror movie – he's back. Only this time – he's not running Scotland. He would have the decisive say in running a country he wants to see abolished – our United Kingdom.

Isn't it appalling that Labour won't rule out this outcome, that they would wrap themselves in the flag one minute and the next be prepared to work with a bunch of people who would rip up that flag given half a chance? Spineless. Weak. Unprincipled. Short-termist. That, my friends, is all anyone needs to know about today's Labour party.

But what about us? Yes, we have a great record in Government, we've got a strong team, but what matters most is our plan for the future. And this has got to be up in lights from the Highlands to the Borders. It's a plan to secure a better future for everyone in Scotland – and it starts with getting Britain back in the black.

This is the country of prudence. Of thrift. You know and I know that sound finances are the rock on which everything else depends – every teacher in every school, every police officer on our streets, every operation in every hospital.

Listen to this: last year we spent over £36 billion on servicing Labour's debt – just on the interest alone and that would have paid for three years of the NHS in Scotland. Our opponents bleat on about 'austerity' but I tell you – if we don't grip these debts, they will grip us and there will be less and less money for our schools, hospitals, communities, pensions – for everything that makes life worthwhile.

So we have set out a clear plan. Balancing the books by 2018. Running a surplus. Fixing the roof while the sun is shining – so we're more protected from future shocks. Britain will be back in the black and holding its head high. And when we get there – when we reach that summit after some long and hard years, we'll be able to look our children and grandchildren in the eye and know we did the right thing.

You know, last week the First Minister gave a speech saying it was 'morally unjustifiable' to continue to restrain spending. I'll tell you what is 'morally unjustifiable', First Minister and that is racking up more debt than our children and grandchildren could ever hope to re-pay, passing the buck like every other hopeless left-wing administration in history and that's why it will be us – the Conservative Party – who will do the right thing, clear up this mess – and leave Scotland standing taller.

Scottish Greens

The Scottish Greens are one of the youngest parties contesting seats at the 2015 UK general election. It was created in 1990 when the former Green Party split into separate parties for Scotland, Northern Ireland and England & Wales. So, unlike the Scottish Labour, Conservative and Liberal Democrat parties, the Scottish Greens are an entirely autonomous party, so much so that many of its members support independence for Scotland and campaigned for a Yes vote in the recent referendum.

Although the old UK Green Party performed relatively well at the 1989 elections to the European Parliament, it was not until the Scottish Parliament was established in 1999 that Greens secured their first parliamentarian in the UK (although George MacLeod had represented the UK Green Party in the House of Lords). That was Robin Harper, who had tried and failed to become a Scottish MEP in 1989.

At the 2003 elections to the Scottish Parliament six more Greens joined Harper as MSPs, although that fell to two in 2007 and remained at that level in 2011. At the 2010 UK general election, meanwhile, the Green Party in England and Wales won its first MP, Caroline Lucas in Brighton. When the SNP formed a minority Scottish Government in 2007 the two Scottish Green MSPs (Robin Harper and Patrick Harvie) voted for Alex Salmond as First Minister.

Although Harper and subsequently Harvie were usually identified as 'leader' of their party, the Scottish Greens in fact have two co-leaders, currently Harvie and Edinburgh City Councillor Maggie Chapman (Natalie Bennett is sole leader of the English & Welsh party). At the May 2015 general election the Scottish Greens plan to contest 31 Scottish constituencies and campaign on higher employment, tackling inequality (via a £10 minimum wage and rolling back welfare cuts with a wealth tax), keeping public services in public hands (opposing TTIP and nationalising the railways), strengthening workers' rights and reforming Westminster (it believes the first-past-the-post system is broken).

The Scottish Green Party's website says it 'is part of an international movement guided by the principles of environmental, social and economic justice'. Furthermore, it favours 'local control, radical participatory democracy and [a commitment] to international co-operation and peaceful means to achieve our objectives'. The website also sets out in greater detail the party's economic policies:

- **Equality not poverty.** We will make a clean break from austerity to create a more equal society and job-rich economy... rather than prioritising growth at all costs, Greens believe that economic policy should also take quality of life into account – things such as our health, our relationships, our rights and our sense of community.

- **Supporting workers.** We will increase the Minimum Wage to the Living Wage... to tackle the worst pay inequality we will link directors' pay to a multiple of their lowest paid employees. We will defend workers' rights to collective bargaining and roll back anti trade union laws. We will work to end discrimination in the workplace through strengthening legislation and education. No-one will be forced into the insecurity of a zero-hours contract and access to employment tribunals will once again be free to workers.

- **Green jobs and enterprise.** We need a transition to a jobs-rich economy which respects the environment and provides for us all. We will deliver a government-led Green New Deal to invest millions of pounds in sustainable jobs and enterprise. We will support sustainable expansion in industries such as great quality food production, clean chemical sciences, digital and creative industries, medical and life sciences, construction, energy efficiency, engineering and the low carbon energy industry... we will invest in apprenticeships, colleges and universities, and invest in research and innovation.

- **Equality not poverty.** In order to ensure a fairer and more equal society, Greens believe that the universal approach to benefits must be defended. We will roll back welfare cuts founded on false claims that people prefer benefits rather than rewarding work. We will abolish the Bedroom Tax and Workfare, lift the punitive sanction regime, halt the roll-out of Universal Credit and allow the Scottish Parliament to design a scheme that works with new devolved social security powers... A Citizen's Income will require a reform programme replacing almost all benefits apart from disability payments with a simple regular payment to everyone – children, adults and pensioners.

- **Banks and finance.** The banking system must serve everyone, and do so fairly. To this end we will encourage a variety of financial institutions, including mutuals, credit unions, and local or regional banks...

> We will support the creation of small local banks with
> a centralised, efficient infrastructure. A National
> Investment Bank will be created to invest in activities
> benefiting all of Scotland's communities while
> respecting ecological limits.[1]

Writing in a newspaper recently, Patrick Harvie said the Scottish Greens would 'be going into this election determined to offer not only clear Green policies, but a new way of doing politics too', standing 'in the majority of seats for the first time ever, and working with our colleagues in the Green Party of England and Wales we'll offer people the chance to vote for what they really believe in.' He continued:

> We'll tell people who welcome a moratorium on
> fracking but also see the need to stop indulging the
> rest of the fossil fuel industry, that they don't need to
> vote for a half measure. We'll tell people who don't
> only want the NHS protected from TTIP but who want
> the whole of that dangerous trade deal killed off, that
> they can elect MPs who will say so. We'll tell people
> who oppose Trident but also oppose NATO that they
> can vote in line with that belief. And we'll tell people
> who want truly radical new powers for Scotland that
> they don't need to hold their noses and vote to use
> those powers to give even bigger corporate tax cuts
> than the UK.

1 http://www.scottishgreens.org.uk/policy/economy/#sthash.
osUNDpsH.dpuf

Natalie Bennett, addressing the Green Party Autumn Conference, 5 September 2014

The Green Party has the policies to ensure that workers are fairly rewarded for their labours. We need jobs that individuals can build their life around: jobs that will pay the rent, pay the food bill, let people think about settling down, start a family, with a reasonable sense of security and hope.

We're long-term proponents of the living wage but we say we need to go further to deliver dignity, security and a fair reward for workers' labour. That's why we're calling for a £10 per hour minimum wage for everyone by 2020.

We're also backing a complete ban zero-hours contracts. No employer should be able to hold their staff captive in a life of uncertainty and fear, subject to the whims and favouritism of managers, with no way of planning how to pay their bills. The zero-hours contract is the return of the Great Depression's street corner queues for work – and we say NO!

We say that public sector workers must not be made to pay for the errors and fraud of the bankers with continued austerity that's hit our dinner ladies, our teachers, our nurses, our firefighters. Money collected from making rich individuals and big businesses can fund the decent, essential public services that we all need.

And the Green Party has policies to restore generational justice – we have policies for the young, the old, and everyone in-between to help them live a life of decent security, a life without fear, in a society that works for the common good.

Now our young people are trapped. We want to set them free. As a society, a country, we have to ensure that the young will not go through decades of life worn down by the weight of student debt. Education is a public good. Whether it's an NVQ or a PhD – makes our society a little stronger, adds to the common good. That's why we demand the complete removal of university tuition fees.

And we'll ensure that private landlords are NOT allowed to continue to charge extortionate rents for rabbit hutches. Our smart rent cap, combined with long-term rental contracts, will keep rent rises down. And we're demanding a living rent commission, to work out how to bring rents back in line with incomes. By abolishing right to buy and freeing councils to borrow to build more council housing – which we so desperately need – we can start to restore the balance to our housing that's not now working for the common good but for a few rich landlords.

And we'll ensure that the disabled and the ill don't have to live in fear of the withdrawal of essential support, support that should be their right, that should be given gladly to those in need in a civilised society. We'll abolish the work capability assessment, acknowledging that the best person to decide on ability to work is that individual's medical practitioner, and restore the level of the former disability living allowance to what's needed, not what the government decides it wants to cut it to.

The Green Party will ensure that no one need fear going hungry, need dread destitution, need face the panic of having nothing. That's the promise, the hope, the brilliance of the basic or citizens' income – that long-term Green Party policy that's now taking an increasing prominent place in the thinking of campaigners here in Britain and around the world.

And, most fundamentally of all, the Green Party's are the policies that recognise that our economy is a subset of the natural environment. There are no jobs on a dead planet. There is no life as we know it on a 6-degree-warmed world.

The Green Alliance of environmental charities and campaigners – together they represent 7 million people – just this week rightly said that we need a plan to restore our natural environment. It's being depleted by the hour – the greenbelt concreted over, the soil and water poisoned with noxious chemicals, our seas sterilised by disastrous fishing methods.

We need action. We need to rein in the agrochemical companies, the factory farmers and the developers. Greens have been leading in the struggle to ban chemicals being broadcast into our environment without understanding of the consequences, not just for bees, but for many other species. We're leading in the struggle to protect the green belt. And we're encouraging the small-scale, local agriculture that we need to provide food security – and jobs and business opportunities – in our future, not the disastrous, damaging industrial agriculture that's producing green deserts across our land, killing off our farmland birds, our hedgehogs, and our soils.

And we need an energy policy, not the disastrous mishmash this government has delivered. We need to commit, now, to a zero-carbon electricity future – there are so many exciting possibilities for wind, solar, and tidal. We need to power up now. And for transport we need to invest for the future – not the back-of-an-envelope HS2 plan, but support for walking and cycling, for local buses, and local trains. Real change here doesn't just deliver for the environment, it also delivers in people's lives – cutting their costs, letting them sit back relax on their journeys. The only downside may be that our social media gets even busier, but congestion in the virtual world beats congestion and pollution in the real one.

I want to make one final reflection on the work that lies ahead of us, before we get back to the important democratic deliberations of the conference. Since 2010, the foundations of the Green Party have become a lot stronger, our support is growing fast. And the political landscape has changed.

We can make 2015 the year the Green Party cements itself as a core block, a central element, of British political life. We've long been creating the policies that other eventually 'steal' as their own. We've long been the trailblazers who encouraged the braver members of other parties to push their leadership towards action. We've long been the people who asked the tough questions, pointed out the social and environmental flaws in policies.

But increasingly we're being – and we're determined to be – elected, to be in the position to put our policies for real change into action. The general election in 2015 is a big challenge, and a huge opportunity. I invite you all to join me in seizing it. Let's do it!

Scottish Labour Party

4

Until recently the Scottish Labour Party was consistently the largest party in Scotland regardless of election results across the UK as a whole. Certainly that was the case at every UK general election after and including 1959, while even as recently as 2010 the party increased its share of the vote in Scotland by three per cent, despite a swing against it in England & Wales (like the Conservatives, Labour does not contest seats in Northern Ireland).

As observed in the introduction, judging by several pre-election opinion polls that position of dominance now appears to be under threat from the Scottish National Party (SNP). Indeed, the challenge faced by the Scottish Labour Party first manifested itself in elections to the Scottish Parliament. Although Labour (in coalition with the Liberal Democrats) formed the first two devolved Scottish Executives in 1999–2003 and 2003–7, in both the 2007 and 2011 Holyrood elections its share of the vote and number of MSPs declined.

Leading the Scottish Labour Party into the 2015 general election is Jim Murphy, MP for the Westminster constituency of East Renfrewshire since 1997. Although he will seek re-election in May, Murphy also intends to stand for the Scottish Parliament at the election due in May 2016. Since becoming leader in late 2014 he has repeatedly asserted his independence from UK Labour leader Ed Miliband, and while the Scottish Labour Party recently acquired more operational autonomy from the London-based organisation, the two will campaign together closely at the forthcoming contest.

At a one-day conference in Edinburgh in March 2015 the Scottish Labour Party also revised its constitution, which now states:

The Scottish Labour Party is a democratic socialist party rooted in social justice... [and] to these ends we work for the patriotic interest of the people of Scotland:

– For the success of a permanent and powerful Scottish Parliament.

– Decisions on policy that is devolved to the Scottish Parliament will be decided by the Scottish Labour Party.

– In common purpose with all parts of the Labour Party and Labour Movement across the UK for the advancement of Scotland's interests and the benefit of all.

– With the Scottish people to create policy in Scotland for a just society, a prosperous economy, a vibrant cultural life, and a more sustainable, democratic Scotland.

– With others, across the UK and internationally, to unlock the potential of all and to create a fairer society.

On the basis of these principles, adds the revised constitution, 'Scottish Labour seeks the trust of the Scottish people to govern'.

Across the UK the Labour Party is fighting the 2015 general election on five main pledges under the slogan 'A better plan. A better future.' These are:

- **A strong economic foundation**. We will balance the books and cut the deficit every year while securing the future of the NHS. None of our manifesto commitments require additional borrowing.

- **Higher living standards for working families**. We will freeze energy bills until 2017 and give the regulator the power to cut bills this winter. We will ban exploitative zero-hours contracts, raise the minimum wage to £8, and provide 25 hours free childcare.

- **An NHS with the time to care**. We will build an NHS with the time to care: 20,000 more nurses and 8,000 more GPs. We will join up services from home to hospital, and guarantee GP appointments within 48 hours and cancer tests within one week.

- **Controls on immigration**. People who come here won't be able to claim benefits for at least two years, and we will introduce fair rules making it illegal for employers to undercut wages by exploiting workers.

- **A country where the next generation can do better than the last**. We will reduce tuition fees [in England and Wales] to £6,000, guarantee an apprenticeship for every school leaver who gets the basic grades, and ensure smaller class sizes for 5, 6, & 7-year-olds.[1]

When it comes to Scotland, since January 2015 Jim Murphy has unveiled a series of 'election pledges'. The first promised to fund 1,000 'extra' nurses for Scotland, funded from the UK-wide 'Mansion Tax' (the party calculates that up to 95 per cent of revenue generated by the new property tax would come from the south-east of England, amounting to £250 million for Scotland). Furthermore, Murphy said it would deliver funding 'for more nurses over and above anything the SNP propose'.[2]

1   http://www.labour.org.uk/pledges
2   http://www.scottishlabour.org.uk/blog/entry/scottish-labours-first-election-pledge-1000-new-nurses-for-scotland

Scottish Labour's second election pledge, meanwhile, committed to giving the Scottish Parliament the 'final say' over benefits. This meant the party was moving beyond the so-called 'Vow' that had resulted in the cross-party Smith Commission recommendations on more powers for Holyrood. Speaking alongside former Labour Prime Minister Gordon Brown, Jim Murphy said his party, if elected, would go 'further' than The Vow and Smith in five 'important areas':

- **Giving the Scottish Parliament a power to top up benefits.**
- **Ensuring our Parliament has the power to create new benefits.**
- **Bringing employment and welfare policy together in Scotland.**
- **Full devolution of housing benefit.**
- **Devolving welfare not just to Holyrood but to local communities.**

More generally the Scottish Labour Party has focused on 'redistribution', which it says differentiates it from both the Conservatives and the SNP, thus it proposes using some of the proceeds of a 50p top rate of tax (levied on incomes of more than £150,000) to tackle educational disadvantage. Jim Murphy has committed to maintaining free tuition fees in Scotland, which reversed the Scottish Labour Party's previous position (and policy between 1999 and 2007) of a graduate endowment payable upon graduation. Scottish Labour also says it will double the number of classroom assistants in primaries associated with the 'most challenging' 20 secondary schools, although that is a devolved policy area.

On the economy, Scottish Labour's pitch is 'making the economy work for working people'. It claims to offer an alternative to Conservative 'austerity' (although other parties, such as the SNP, dispute that) with plans to boost productivity and reforming the labour market in order to tackle low pay. Jim Murphy spoke about this in greater detail in a speech to the David Hume Institute in Edinburgh,[3] setting out plans to raise the minimum wage, promote a 'living wage', ban zero-hour contracts and using a tax on bonuses in the financial services sector to 'guarantee' young people a job or training.

In terms of the constitution, the party continues to oppose – as it did during the referendum – independence, but supports more autonomy within the UK. Scottish Labour has also made much of the SNP's commitment to what it calls devo-max or 'full fiscal autonomy' for Scotland, which it says would 'bin' the Barnett Formula and thus leave the Scottish Government vulnerable to the 'uncertainty' of fluctuations in North Sea oil revenue. More broadly, Jim Murphy says that in May 2015 Scots 'face a choice': 'We can send SNP MPs to protest against the Tory Government, or we can send Scottish Labour MPs to replace a Tory Government.' He added:

> A vote for the SNP means risking another five years of the Tories. Only Labour is big enough and strong enough across the UK to kick [David] Cameron out of Number 10... So often in politics we hear from voters that politicians are all the same or from commentators that the differences between parties are marginal. But

3   http://www.davidhumeinstitute.com/images/stories/Seminars/ Winter_Series_2015/Speech_by_Jim_Murphy_MP.pdf

this is a uniquely Labour pledge for a Labour priority. Scotland has two parties telling it that they are powerless to make this sort of change. For the Tories the excuse is the deficit. For the nationalists the excuse is the union. If they can't make a difference then they should move over for people who can. I don't think people want to hear excuses anymore. 2014 was a year when Scotland cried out for change. 2015 must be the year when we answer that call for change.[4]

4   http://www.scottishlabour.org.uk/blog/entry/scottish-labours-first-election-pledge-1000-new-nurses-for-scotland

Ed Miliband MP, speech to the Fabians Conference, 17 January 2015

Britain needs a new plan. To address our economic problems. A plan based on a fundamentally different idea. The idea that if you put working people first, then Britain as a whole will do well, both now and in the future. That's what Labour offers in this general election.

Each day, each week, each month, the beating heart of the Labour government will be the fortunes of working people. So we will balance the books and cut the deficit every year but not by shredding our public services. Instead, we will make common sense reductions in spending, with departmental spending falling outside protected areas.

But we know that you can't simply cut your way to deficit reduction. So we will also make sure that everyone pays their fair share: we will repeal this government's tax cut for millionaires and introduce a Mansion Tax, on houses above £2 million. And most importantly of all we will cut the deficit with the different kind of economy we need for working people: higher skills, higher productivity, therefore higher revenues.

A race to the top, not a race to the bottom, in wages and conditions. We will end the scandal of exploitative zero-hours contracts. We will raise the minimum wage to over £8 an hour. And to create the country we believe in, to build that future, young people will be at the heart of our plan.

We judge the ethics of a country by whether it gives dignity to those in old age. We judge the future of a country by the prospects for the young. Now, I don't think there has ever been a government that has so often made the young pay the price for hard times than this one. We will have a new direction.

An education system that serves every child in our country: creative, inspiring. And doing what our country has never done: valuing vocational and academic qualifications equally. Every young person deserves a chance of a decent education after 18 and a career.

And we need to be doing the right thing by the next generation and the generation after that, by putting climate change at the centre of the agenda. Not just for the environment, but in our plan for our economy and the jobs of the future.

To make this plan for working people work, we need every part of our society playing their part from top to bottom. The powerful interests that had things their own way finally held to account. Let's have the fight about who will best stand up to the energy companies. A Tory party that stands by as people are ripped off month after month, year after year. Or a Labour plan that gives regulator the power to cut prices, with an energy price freeze until 2017 to ensure prices can only fall and cannot rise.

We will break up the big banks and get proper competition on the high street and create a British Investment bank, with regional banks in every single part of the country. And those fair rules shouldn't just apply to the powerful. Everyone should play by them. Including people who come to live and work in Britain from abroad. Immigration makes us stronger, richer and more powerful as a nation. But making immigration work for everyone and not just a few, means people should contribute before they claim and we should never, ever allow companies to undercut wages and conditions of workers here by paying slave wages to those brought in from overseas.

An open, tolerant Britain is the way we succeed in our economy and in our society. An open, tolerant Britain inside not outside the European Union. If you want to know what a real threat to prosperity looks like, think about a Conservative government sleepwalking to the exit door of the European Union.

Finally, our plan will transform our public services for the 21st century, even in tough times. Including our National Health Service. We're a country where in the last two weeks, we've seen a treatment tent erected in a hospital car park, ambulances queuing up outside hospitals and a patient being treated in a store cupboard. It is shameful. David Cameron should be ashamed. He has betrayed people's trust on our NHS. The British people will never trust him again.

And what you will see from Labour is plans for public health, for mental health and our ten year plan for the future of health and social care. Not a plan for the NHS to stand still but a plan to improve the service for the future. Because the only way to solve the A&E crisis inside our hospitals, is by improving services at home and in the community. Access to GPs. Care for the elderly. A 21st century health and social care service.

And it is right not just to have Mansion Tax, but to raise new revenue from the tobacco companies and clampdown on tax avoidance by the hedge funds, for more midwives, care workers, doctors and nurses. Because those with the broadest shoulders should bear the greatest burden and we need a NHS with time to care. And it will be a NHS run on the right principles of care, compassion and cooperation, not competition, privatisation and fragmentation.

And that's why we will repeal this government's Health and Social Care Act. This is a plan that can change things for our country. A plan that can make Britain a world leader in the campaign to tackle the greatest 21st century challenge of inequality and an economy that doesn't work for everyday people. It is a plan that can bring real, enduring prosperity to every part of Britain.

But it is not a plan that is going to happen automatically. It will require a new way of doing things. As well as tackling inequalities of income and wealth, we will tackle inequalities of power. Because it is right thing to do. And it is the only way to make our plan work. All sources of power – private and public – should be accountable. That means at local level, health, education and policing should be accountable to local people. And they will be.

And it means we take power and resources out of Whitehall, with a comprehensive, not a piecemeal, plan for city and county regions, over economic development, transport and skills. A £30 billion devolution of spending to local people. It is time to devolve power and reverse a century of centralisation. And just as the only way to govern is by sharing power, so too the only way to win is with the power of our movement.

Scottish Liberal Democrats

5

The Scottish Liberal Democrats are still a relatively young political party, certainly compared with Labour and the Conservatives. At the same time it grew out of a 1988 merger between two separate parties, the historic Scottish Liberal Party and the Social Democratic Party in Scotland (formed in 1981). Structurally, the Scottish Liberal Democrats forms one of three parts of the federal UK Liberal Democrats, the others being the parties in Wales and England.

Since the late 1980s the party consistently campaigned for a devolved Scottish Parliament (especially alongside Labour and the Greens as part of the Scottish Constitutional Convention, which reported in the early 1990s), while at the devolution referendum held in September 1997 the Scottish Liberal Democrats campaigned with the SNP and Labour for a Yes-Yes vote to a devolved parliament with tax-varying powers. It was fitting, therefore, that the party formed the first Scottish Executive in coalition with Labour following the first elections to the Scottish Parliament in May 1999.

The period between 1999 and 2007 represented the party's high point, during which it helped implement a number of long-standing Liberal Democrat policies, most notably the abolition of up-front tuition fees and the introduction of a Single Transferable Vote electoral system for Scottish local government. Jim Wallace, the party's leader (and Deputy First Minister) for most of that period, was also recognised as an effective minister, deputising for successive First Ministers on several occasions.

The Holyrood elections in 2007, however, marked the beginning of a period of electoral decline. Several observers believed the party's refusal to enter a coalition with the SNP (the Scottish Liberal Democrats refused to support holding a referendum on independence) was a strategic mistake and, in 2010, when the UK Liberal Democrats entered a coalition with the Conservatives, the Scottish party began to lose support. At the Holyrood elections in 2011 just five Scottish Liberal Democrat MSPs were elected, losing all its mainland constituencies.

In the run up to the Scottish independence referendum in September 2014 the Scottish Liberal Democrats – like the Scottish Conservatives and Scottish Labour Party – campaigned for a No vote, while also renewing its commitment to more devolution for Scotland within a 'federal' United Kingdom. Sir Menzies Campbell, a former UK party leader, chaired a policy commission on more powers, and the Scottish Liberal Democrats took part in the cross-party Smith Commission after the referendum.

Across Scotland and as part of the UK government the Scottish Liberal Democrats say they have helped 'build a stronger economy and a fairer society, enabling everyone to get on in life'. It lists its achievements since the last UK general election as:

- **Taxes down.** £800 back in the pockets of more than 2 million Scots on low and middle incomes thanks to Liberal Democrat income tax plans.

- **Pensions up.** Record cash increases to the state pension of more than 890,000 older people in Scotland thanks to the Liberal Democrat pensions 'triple lock'.

- **New jobs.** More than 130,000 new jobs across Scotland since 2010, record employment levels across the UK and the fastest economic growth rate in the G7.

- **More childcare.** Successfully pressed the Scottish Government to match Lib Dem action on childcare that will see thousands of families receive 15 hours of free care this year, and a new £1,200 tax break for parents to help give their child the best start in life.

- **A stronger Scotland.** Delivered big new powers for the Scottish Parliament and leading the debate on building a stronger Scotland within the United Kingdom.

In February this year the leader of the Scottish Liberal Democrats, Willie Rennie MSP, and the former UK party leader Charles Kennedy MP set out six 'priorities' that would form the basis of its 2015 general election manifesto. It said these commitments were 'only possible' because of its strategy 'to deliver a balanced budget', borrow 'less than Labour' and cut 'less than the Conservatives'. The six priorities were:

- **Prosperity for all.** Balance the budget fairly and invest to build a high skill, low carbon economy.

- **Fair taxes.** Cut your taxes by an additional £400 by raising the tax-free allowance to £12,500.

- **Quality healthcare for all.** Invest £8bn to improve our NHS and guarantee equal care for mental health.

- **Opportunity for every child.** Guarantee education funding from nursery to college.

- **Our environment protected**. Protect nature and fight climate change with five Green Laws.
- **A stronger Scotland for everyone**. Transfer power from London to Scotland with home rule in the UK.

Speaking in Fort William, Willie Rennie said:

> In Government, the Liberal Democrats have delivered on the front page of our previous General Election manifesto. Liberal Democrats have made the weather on more powers, whilst Scotland's lowest paid are no longer paying Income Tax. We will build on this progress. Whether you live in our cities or our countryside, work in our hospitals or our oil rigs, bring up your family in the Highlands or the Borders, voted Yes or No, I know we all want to see a stronger Scotland. We will deliver real home rule to Scotland through the Smith Agreement. But more than that, we will build a stronger economy and a fairer society by ensuring decent local services.[1]

1   www.scotlibdems.org.uk/rennie_and_kennedy_launch_manifesto_front_page

Nick Clegg MP, speech to Scottish Liberal Democrat conference, Aberdeen, 20 March 2015

In England, the NHS needs an extra £8bn a year by 2020 in order to do that. That is what they have told us they need. Yet we are the only party to commit to it. Not Labour, not the Conservatives. That commitment means an extra £800m a year for the health service in Scotland – money that is desperately needed but no other party is prepared to give.

Of course, it is up to the Scottish government whether it chooses to spend that money on the Scottish NHS or not. But that is exactly where I, and Willie, believe it must be spent. And it must be spent on Scottish health priorities. You have rightly campaigned against the SNP's neglect of the health service that has led to the A&E crisis.

And I am very glad that, just as we have in Westminster, you are fighting to improve mental health services in Scotland. For too long, mental health has been treated as a Cinderella service, neglected and under-funded. The consequences have been devastating for millions of people. One in four of us will suffer a mental health condition at some point in our lives. One in four. Three children in every classroom has a mental health condition. That is unacceptable in modern Britain.

We have started the work of undoing the neglect of mental health services in England but it cannot be done overnight. The Scottish Government must do the same. They can start by putting £25m a year into mental health services for children and young people. That is the money Scotland will receive as a result of us investing to improve these vital services in England in this week's Budget.

Conference, this is a liberal mission. We must not allow people to be denied the support, treatment and opportunity they need to get better and live healthy, productive lives. And we must work every day to end the devastating stigma that surrounds mental health. That is why I am so incredibly proud that we are the first party to put equality for people with mental health problems on the front page of our manifesto.

We have shown incredible resilience in the last five years. And that resilience has allowed us to do incredible things. Secure the economic recovery. Cut taxes for working people. Improve mental health services. Give pensioners dignity in retirement. Deliver home rule for Scotland.

And it is because of that resilience that we can and will win this May. That resilience will see off the SNP challenge in the seats we hold. And it will wipe the smile off Alex Salmond's face in Gordon too. At least then he will have another defeat to write a book about. I've heard the predictions. I've seen the polls. But let me tell you this: we will do so much better than anyone thinks. In those seats where we are out in force, making our case loudly and proudly, we are the ones making the weather.

I've seen it for myself in Liberal Democrat seats across the country – and it is just as true in Scotland as it is everywhere else. We are showing that with hard work, strong local campaigns and a record of delivering for people in Westminster, Holyrood and communities across Scotland, we can and will win. It won't be easy, but winning shouldn't be.

We need to persuade people every day between now and 7 May that their lives will be better with Liberal Democrat councillors making a difference in their communities, Liberal Democrat MPs and MSPs fighting their corner in Westminster and Holyrood, and Liberal Democrat ministers serving them in Government. Every Liberal Democrat elected in May makes our voice louder.

So get out there and tell people what we have done to help them and their community. No one else will do it for us. Tell them how we have fought their corner in Holyrood and Westminster. Tell them what we have done to build a stronger economy and a fairer society. And tell that the Liberal Democrats are the only party that will keep Britain on track and govern for the whole country. Do that and we can and will win.

Scottish National Party

6

In the context of contemporary UK politics, the Scottish National Party (SNP) needs little introduction. Formed back in 1934 as a result of a merger between the 'Scottish Party' and 'National Party of Scotland', as its website says, the party 'has been at the forefront of the campaign for Scottish independence for over seven decades'.

Since forming a minority Scottish Government in 2007, that goal has dominated Scottish and UK politics, a far cry from the SNP's status a quarter of a century ago. Then, it was regarded as an ill-disciplined fringe political party that presented little threat to the much larger, and Unionist, Labour Party. But after a young MP called Alex Salmond became party leader in 1990, the SNP began to professionalise and gradually increase its electoral support.

At times, however, it looked as if the creation of a Scottish Parliament in 1999 had, as the Scottish Labour MP George Robertson once memorably predicted, had killed Nationalism 'stone dead'. Although the SNP became the main opposition party, Alex Salmond stood down as leader in 2000 and the party lost support at each Scottish, UK and European election over the next few years.

Only when Alex Salmond made a surprise return as leader in 2004 – with the SNP MSP Nicola Sturgeon as his deputy – did the party's fortunes begin to improve and, in May 2007, it formed a minority administration at Holyrood. Four years later it won a landslide majority, and three years after that a referendum on Scottish independence – the SNP's aim since the year 2000 – was held at the end of a long-running and energetic debate about Scotland's constitutional future.

Although the Yes campaign did not win (it secured 45 per cent of the vote) and Alex Salmond announced his resignation as SNP leader the following day, the party continued to go from strength to strength, not only quadrupling its membership but gathering support in several opinion polls. In November 2014 Nicola Sturgeon became the SNP's new leader (unopposed) and, therefore, First Minister of Scotland, and she, like her predecessor, enjoyed remarkably high approval ratings.

Historically, the SNP had usually ended up getting 'squeezed' in Westminster elections. In other words, most Scottish voters did not see the point of supporting a party that could not obtain a UK-wide majority and thus generally supported the Scottish Labour Party. Since the 1980s the SNP had argued that a large number of MPs (the most it has ever secured is 11 in October 1974) could hold the 'balance of power' in the House of Commons, but only after the 2010 general election, which produced a 'hung' Parliament, did that claim look credible.

In the context of the 2015 general election Nicola Sturgeon has made it very clear that under no circumstances would the SNP support (either formally or informally) a UK Conservative government, although she has spoken of supporting Ed Miliband's Labour Party on an issue-by-issue basis (both Sturgeon and Miliband have ruled out a formal coalition). The SNP has also promoted the idea of a 'progressive alliance' at Westminster, whereby the SNP, Plaid Cymru and Greens (in England and Wales) would collaborate to promote and vote on 'progressive' policies. Alex Salmond, who is bidding to become an MP again having left the House of Commons in 2010, has spoken of 'shaking up' Westminster, although Sturgeon has promised a 'constructive' approach.

Beyond a broad aim of playing an influential role in next UK Parliament, the SNP aims to have an impact on a number of policy areas still 'reserved' to Westminster. These are as follows:

- **Economy.** The SNP will offer an 'alternative to austerity' by limiting real-terms growth in departmental spending to 0.5 per cent each year in order to permit a further £180 billion of investment across the UK over the next four years. It will also support 'fairer increases in the minimum wage' and suggest 'improvements' to the Smith Commission so that the Scottish Parliament can 'create jobs and tackle inequality'. Finally, the SNP would make support for the oil and gas sector 'a key election priority' (it supports a moratorium on planning consents for unconventional onshore oil & gas, including fracking), while supporting the use of large-scale infrastructure projects to maximise economic growth in Scotland and across the UK.

- **Foreign policy/defence.** The SNP will 'oppose the renewal of Trident nuclear weapons' and 'fight to protect our conventional defence forces from further Westminster cuts'. Furthermore, it is calling for publication of the Chilcot report into the causes of the war in Iraq before the general election on 7 May, arguing for an 'ethical' foreign policy ('one which advances the cause of peace and justice, not war and occupation') and believes that a United Nations target of spending 0.7 per cent of Gross National Income on international aid ought to be enshrined in law.

- **Europe**. The SNP says it understands and supports 'the case for reform but believe that this is best achieved from within the European Union'. It also argues that for the UK to leave the EU it 'should require not just a majority across the whole UK but a majority in each one of the four nations'. The SNP believe Scotland would be best represented in the EU as an independent nation with its 'own seat at the top table', allowing the Scottish Government to represent Scotland's interests in areas like fisheries while developing 'strong partnerships with like-minded European partners to secure tangible benefit for Scotland'. The SNP would oppose any attempt by a future UK Government to withdraw from the European Arrest Warrant.

- **Immigration**. The SNP believes the Scottish Government should have full control over immigration policy in order to meet Scotland's 'population and economic needs, while enriching our society'. It would also reintroduce the post-study work visa, lower the current financial maintenance thresholds and minimum salary levels for entry.

- **Welfare**. The SNP will continue to argue that responsibility for all benefits and tax credits should be devolved to the Scottish Parliament, while it wants to halt roll-out of Personal Independence Payments (which replace Disability Living Allowance) and the Universal Credit in Scotland, while scrapping the so-called Bedroom Tax. The Basic State Pension and the new single-tier pension, meanwhile, should be protected by the triple-lock for the whole of the next Parliament.

- **Democracy**. The SNP says it supports enabling 16 and 17 year olds to vote in all Scottish elections, while it will 'never take seats in the unelected House of Lords', which it believes 'should be abolished and replaced with a democratic institution accountable to the electorate'. The party 'strongly' opposes any attempt by a future UK Government to repeal the Human Rights Act or to withdraw from the European Convention on Human Rights.

- **Health**. The SNP says it will be prepared to support a Bill in the House of Commons which would 'restore the National Health Service in England to the accountable public service it was always meant to be, and consequentially protect Scotland's NHS budget from the spectre of austerity, privatisation and patient charging in England'.

For more information, please see www.snp.org

Nicola Sturgeon MSP, speech at University College London, 11 February 2015

The Chancellor is making unprecedented cuts to public spending and the public services on which we all rely. He is doing so in the name of fiscal responsibility. Yet his entire economic model depends on individual households taking on more debt than at any time in history. Instead of pooling risk, the government is dispersing it to households across the country. Individuals will be deeper in debt, families will feel less secure, the economy will be less resilient. It's morally unjustifiable and economically unsustainable.

The Scottish Government proposes a different approach... In terms of the UK economy, we believe that debt should be reduced as a percentage of GDP – but more gradually than either of the largest UK parties is proposing. For example if you limited real terms growth in departmental spending to half a per cent each year – it would reduce debt as a share of GDP in every year from 2016–17. But it would also permit – compared to current UK government plans – a further £180 billion of investment across the UK over the next four years.

We could protect the infrastructure, education and innovation which will support stronger and more sustainable growth in the future. And we could take a different approach to the crude cuts that reduce work incentives and impact directly on disabled people and families with children. We could manage the deficit down, but without destroying the social fabric.

And of course, we could also release savings through some very straightforward choices. Deciding not to renew Trident, for example, would save around £100bn, at 2012 prices, over the next 35 years.

The Trident Commission last year estimated that the equivalent annual cost of a new Trident system will be almost £3bn. Cash costs will peak at £4bn in the mid 2020s. That is money that could be – and should be – invested instead in health and education.

So, by taking a different approach – by offering an alternative to the austerity agenda of both Labour and the Tories – we would ensure that fiscal consolidation is consistent with a wider vision of society. A society which strives to become more equal, as part of becoming more prosperous.

We simply don't accept that there's a trade-off between balancing the books and having a balanced society; fairness and prosperity can go hand in hand. Indeed, I'd put it more strongly – they must go hand in hand.

The Scottish Government's approach is part of a growing international consensus. IMF research – examining 173 countries over 50 years – has shown that more unequal countries tend to have lower and less durable growth.

It's an argument that Mark Carney has endorsed; Christine Lagarde at the IMF has made it very strongly; its principles underpin much of President Obama's economic policy in the USA.

It has profound implications here in the UK – which is currently the 6th most unequal country in the developed world. Scotland on its own fares slightly better – by 9 places – but not well enough.

There is overwhelming evidence that this degree of inequality harms our economy. In fact, the OECD estimated that inequality reduced the UK's economic growth by 9 percentage points between 1990 and 2010. It's basic common sense that as a society, we will do better if we can benefit from the skill, talent and innovation of all of our people.

But there are other reasons too. Higher incomes would increase demand and boost the revenues needed for investment in infrastructure and education. More equal economies are more resilient and less likely to depend on borrowing and credit. That reduces what is called failure demand in public services – meaning the state can spend more effectively on health, welfare and justice...

We [the Scottish Government] have done a pretty good job – in the face of an incredibly difficult economic climate – of protecting growth, improving the long-term potential of the economy and enhancing social justice. In doing so, we've consistently set out an optimistic vision of how we can work together in Scotland, for the common weal or the common good. And one reason why there has been such a consensus in Scotland that the Parliament needs more powers, is that people trust us to use those powers responsibly...

But just at the moment, after a momentous 12 months in Scotland, we will see a hugely significant 12 months across the whole of the UK. And I hope that Scotland can again exert a beneficial and progressive influence on developments here in London.

If we do, we will make the case for a more rational economic policy at Westminster. And we will use the powers we have in the Scottish Parliament to pursue a different approach; one based on partnership, fairness and prosperity. Because if that approach can take root more widely, it will help to halt the deeply misguided march to further austerity at Westminster. And that's something which will bring benefits to Scotland, and to all of the UK.

UK Independence Party

The UK Independence Party, commonly known as UKIP, was founded in 1993 by members of the Anti-Federalist League with the primary objective of securing the UK's withdrawal from membership of the European Union (EU). The party describes itself as a 'democratic, libertarian party' while commentators generally classify it as Eurosceptic, right wing and populist.

UKIP is led by Nigel Farage and his deputy Paul Nuttall. The party currently has two MPs (both gained at by-elections in 2014), three representatives in the House of Lords and 24 Members of the European Parliament (including Farage and Nuttall), making it the largest UK party there. In the 2014 European elections, it gained its first MEP – David Coburn – in Scotland.

UKIP Scotland argues that all the main parties, the Conservatives, Labour, the Liberal Democrats and the Scottish National Party all 'favour further EU integration and interference', while it says the SNP would 'like to break up Great Britain and get rid of rule from Westminster only to hand over that freedom to Brussels'. Although it used to support abolition of the Scottish Parliament, UKIP now supports the creation of a 'federal' UK and 'Swiss-style direct democracy' in order to 'devolve power back to the people'.

According to UKIP Scotland's Facebook page the party 'enthusiastically support the celebration of Scotland and Scottish culture by encouraging the teaching of Gaelic languages and histories in England, Scotland, [Northern] Ireland, Wales and Cornwall'. It would also like to 'end the climate of political correctness and restore a pride in Britishness in an inclusive and tolerant manner for all'.

On 21 February 2015 UKIP Scotland formally launched its general election campaign and said it hoped to field candidates in every Scottish constituency, including MEP David Coburn who will stand in Falkirk. Other candidates include the Aberdeen nurse Emily Santos, who is standing in Gordon, regional organiser Kevin Newton who will fight the Conservative-held Dumfriesshire, Clydesdale and Tweeddale, and UKIP's Scottish chairman Arthur Misty Thackeray, who will be standing in the Labour-held seat of Glasgow East.

Speaking at the campaign launch, David Coburn said he was confident of becoming Scotland's first UKIP MP. 'This is the most unpredictable election in 100 years,' he said. 'People are fed up, people want change, they're fed up of the same old, same old. So I think they're turning to UKIP in droves.' In terms of policies, UKIP Scotland says it will put 're-industrialisation' at the heart of its general election campaign in Scotland, promising to set up a commission to look at ways to rejuvenate and expand Scotland's coal industry, support fracking and abolish subsidies for wind, solar and nuclear power.

At a separate UKIP event in the seaside town of Margate, the party also set out plans to cut billions from Scottish government funding to help 'balance the books' if it has a role in the UK government after 7 May. In a speech, UKIP deputy leader Paul Nuttall identified higher per capita public spending and the absence of 'English Votes for English Laws' in the House of Commons as examples of England being 'punished' by Scottish MPs. He said more devolution as recommended by the Smith Commission would make Scottish MPs 'too powerful', while UKIP's deputy chairwoman Suzanne Evans said that scrapping the Barnett Formula (or equalising per capita public spending between Scotland and England) would save £8 billion.

For more information, please see
www.facebook.com/ukipinscotland

7

Nigel Farage MEP, speech to UK Independence Party conference, 20 September 2013

UKIP is a free-thinking, egalitarian party opposed to racism, sectarianism and extremism. UKIP is dedicated to liberty, opportunity, equality under the law and the aspirations of the British people.

We will always act in the interests of Britain. Especially on immigration, employment, energy supply and fisheries. We know that only by leaving the union can we regain control of our borders, our parliament, democracy and our ability to trade freely with the fastest-growing economies in the world. And £55 million a day, incidentally, we get that back as well. A referendum to allow the country to decide this matter will create the greatest opportunity for national renewal in our lifetime.

That's us. Optimistic. Open to the world. The opposite of insular. Out there trading with countries that have growth rates of six, seven, ten per cent a year. Not hemmed in by the European Union – but open to the Commonwealth. Not headed by my old pal Herman Achille van Rompuy but by the Queen. Our real friends in the Commonwealth.

Because the fact is we just don't belong in the European Union. Britain is different. Our geography puts us apart. Our history puts us apart. Our institutions produced by that history put us apart. We think differently. We behave differently. I'm not giving you the *Love, Actually* version of what makes Britain different.

The roots go back seven, eight, nine hundred years with the Common Law. Civil rights. Habeas corpus. The presumption of innocence. The right to a trial by jury. On the continent – confession is the mother of all evidence. Four years ago, Andrew Symeou was charged with manslaughter on statements extracted by the police and later withdrawn – taken on the European Arrest Warrant, held for ten months in the most appalling conditions, detained in Greece for four years and then walked free when the prosecutor pulled the case. The European Arrest Warrant is an abomination to those of us who care about freedom and justice. And in some sense it was ever thus.

The idea of free speech was a reality in England when Europe was run by princes with tyrannical powers. Throughout Europe, England was known as the land of liberty. Here you had the possibility of dissent. Of free thinking. Independent minds and actions. That's us. UKIP belongs in the mainstream of British political life throughout the centuries.

I always believed since 1999 that Britain was a square peg in the round hole I've come to realize something bigger than that. The union is not just contrary to our interests but contrary to the interests of Europe itself. The Commission has hijacked the institutions of Europe by adopting a flag, an anthem, a president, and through their mad euro project they have driven tens of millions into poverty. Their climate change obsession has destroyed industry across Europe, and their refusal to listen to the people will lead to the very extreme nationalisms the project was supposed to stop.

We are the true Europeans. We want to live and work and breathe and trade in a Europe of democratic nations. But in the last ten or fifteen years this country has seen astonishing change. There has been a phenomenal collapse in national self-confidence. When we signed up to government from the Continent, most Britons didn't know what they were letting themselves in for.

Our laws have come from Brussels – and what laws. What directives. What a list of instructions. How this shall be done. How that shall be regulated. Process and compliance and inspection and regulation are taking over from production and leadership and enterprise. Financial services make up 10 per cent of the economy. It's not just the City of London; it's Southampton as well. Cardiff. Birmingham. Newcastle. And it's insurance. Reinsurance. Stocks and shares. Futures. Commodities. Pension funds.

It is totally irrelevant to this industry whether we have a Labour or a Tory government because their livelihoods are now regulated by a Frenchman who is no friend of ours. Parliament is reduced to the level of a large council. No one knows for sure exactly how much of our law comes from Brussels. Could be 70 or 80 per cent. We have given up our concept of civil rights. Magna Carta, 800th anniversary [in the year of] the general election.

Habeas corpus. Rights of inheritance. And not just for the aristocracy, as time went by. Our civil rights grew and kept pace with the times and expanded through the Common Law into the modern world – Europe has supplanted it with their Human Rights charter. While they can hold Andrew Symeou in Greece on trumped-up charges for four years – we can't deport a rapist and murderer because he has a right to a family life.

How did they do that to us? They lied to us. They had to. We'd never have agreed to it if they told us the truth and asked for our agreement. And it's created a complete charade in our national life. All the parties now talk tough on immigration. David Cameron said he would bring it down to the tens of thousands. There are still half a million people a year coming in. Do you know, I really think they haven't made the connection.

Other Parties

8

The preceding chapters describe parties contesting the 2015 general election in Scotland that already have representation in the UK Parliament, i.e. Members of the House of Commons. Other parties do not have MPs, but obviously aspire to, and often field candidates in certain Scottish constituencies at election time.

British National Party

The Scottish British National Party's Facebook page describes it as 'Anti-EU Anti mass-immigration' and 'pro economics that create jobs with decent wages. Putting Scots and Brits first.' It adds: 'We are a modern Scottish and British political party that has the desire to protect our cultural identity as Scots but also British.'

The Scottish BNP opposes 'mass uncontrolled immigration' and believes the UK ought to be in 'a trade and economic friendship treaty' with other European nations but not part of the current European Union and its commitment to freedom of movement. It also believes that 'British people' should have the 'first option' on council and social housing as well as jobs.

Constitutionally, the Scottish BNP is opposed to Scottish independence, believing that 'Scotland and Scots have a proud history in shaping the United Kingdom and should continue to confidently do so'. It would stop 'much of the foreign aid' sent to other countries, diverting the money 'to help keep pensioners and the disabled warm'. (www.facebook.com/pages/Scottish-BNP/217042518474832)

At the last general election the Scottish BNP fielded 13 candidates in Scotland.

8

Trade Unionist and Socialist Coalition

The Trade Unionist and Socialist Coalition (TUSC) was launched shortly before the 2010 general election and brought together leading figures from the National Union of Rail, Maritime and Transport Workers (RMT), the Public and Commercial Services Union, the Prison Officers Association, the National Union of Teachers and the Fire Brigades Union. At this general election the TUSC has ten candidates standing in Scottish constituencies and 125 across the UK as a whole. Angela McCormick, for example, will be the TUSC candidate in Glasgow North. For more information, please see www.tusc.org.uk

Scottish Socialist Party

The Scottish Socialist Party (SSP) was founded in 1998 and initially did relatively well in Scottish Parliament elections, winning one MSP (Tommy Sheridan) in 1999 and six in 2003 before a prolonged row that followed Sheridan's resignation as SSP leader in 2004. Neither the SSP nor Sheridan's breakaway 'Solidarity' party won any seats at the 2007 Holyrood elections. More recently, the party formed part of the 'Yes Scotland' campaign during the Scottish independence referendum.

According to its website, the SSP 'is built on social solidarity and the spirit of resistance to oppression, injustice and nasty con tricks that strangle communities and people's lives'. Its 'message' for the general election on 7 May is that it is time to move 'to a society which puts people and the planet before greedy profiteers – an independent socialist Scotland'. In policy terms, the SSP favours a £10-an-hour living wage for all, opposition to austerity, cuts to local services and privatisation,

8

the building of 100,000 fully accessible new homes for rent, replacing the Council Tax with an income based alternative called the Scottish Service Tax, the expansion of green energy programmes including wind, solar and hydroelectric generation under public ownership to combat fuel poverty, the nationalisation of railways and making Scottish public transport free, and scrapping Europe's most repressive anti-union laws.

The SSP's preferred option was to present 'Independence Alliance' candidates at this general election, comprising the Scottish Greens, SNP and the SSP. Instead it will fight four constituencies on 7 May (Edinburgh South, Glasgow East, Paisley & Renfrewshire South and Glasgow South West), presenting its 'own unique case for independence' and spelling 'out the extra powers that a progressive Scottish Government could use to improve the lives of most Scots'. For more information, please see www.scottishsocialistvoice.wordpress.com/2015/02/27/ssp-announces-general-election-challenge.

Socialist Labour Party

The former trade union leader Arthur Scargill established the Socialist Labour Party (SLP) in 1996. It advocates economic localism and is in favour of reopening British coalmines, while ideologically it is committed to socialism and acknowledges Clause IV of the Labour Party's old constitution. At the 2010 general election it contested five seats in Scotland. For more information, please see www.socialist-labour-party.org.uk.

Scottish Christian Party

The Scottish Christian Party's Facebook page says the 'time has come for Christians of all denominations to stand up for their beliefs and resist the tide of secularism destroying our country' (www.facebook.com/ScottishChristianParty). It is part of the UK Christian Party and originated as 'Operation Christian Vote', founded by George Hargreaves, a Pentecostal minister and former songwriter, in May 2004. At this election the Scottish Christian Party is fielding four candidates.

Liberal Party

The Liberal Party was formed in 1989 by a group of individuals within the original UK Liberal Party which opposed its merger with the Social Democratic Party to form what eventually became the Liberal Democrats. It still uses the old Liberal Party logo, and at the 2010 general election had one candidate in Scotland. For more information, please see www.liberal.org.uk.

Scottish Communists

The Scottish Communists (not to be confused with the Communist Party of Scotland, which has never fought a parliamentary election) are part of the Communist Party of Britain and, although founded in 1988, traces its origins back to the Communist Party of Great Britain, which was founded in 1920. Constitutionally, it supports what it calls 'progressive federalism' for the UK rather than Scottish independence. At this election Zoe Hennessy is standing on behalf of the Scottish Communists in the Glasgow North West constituency. For more information, please see www.scottishcommunists.org.uk

8

Possible Outcomes

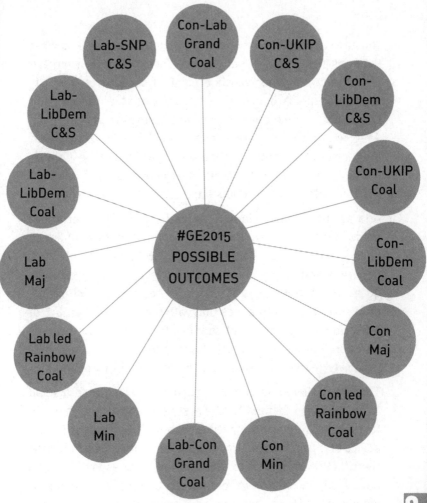

Con-Lab Grand Coal

Con-UKIP C&S

Lab-SNP C&S

Con-LibDem C&S

Lab-LibDem C&S

Con-UKIP Coal

Lab-LibDem Coal

Con-LibDem Coal

#GE2015 POSSIBLE OUTCOMES

Lab Maj

Con Maj

Lab led Rainbow Coal

Con led Rainbow Coal

Lab Min

Lab-Con Grand Coal

Con Min

If none of the above prove sustainable, then another election could take place later in 2015

You have now voted in the 2015 UK general election – so what happens next? Given that the UK does not have a written constitution, in other words a codified account of how it is governed, this is based upon a combination of custom and precedent, i.e. how governments have been formed in the past. A few months after the last general election in 2010, however, the then government published something called the 'Cabinet Manual', which aimed to set out 'the main laws, rules and conventions affecting the conduct and operation of government'.

And as the Cabinet Manual states first off: 'A government holds office by virtue of its ability to command the confidence of the House of Commons, chosen by the electorate in a general election.' By 'command the confidence of' it means a government that enjoys a majority of seats in the Commons, or in certain circumstances that with the greatest number of MPs. So a UK government can be either a 'majority' administration (one or more parties with a majority of seats) or a 'minority' (one or more parties without a majority of seats).

The new Parliament – composed of newly elected or re-elected MPs – also has to meet for the first time, and although this is technically a decision for the Sovereign (the Queen) on the advice of the incumbent Prime Minister, until the last election the practice was for it to meet on the Wednesday following polling day. In 2007, however, a Select Committee on Modernisation of the House of Commons recommended returning to a previous practice of leaving an interval of 12 days between polling day and the first meeting of Parliament. This is what happened in 2010.

When Parliament does meet for the first time following a general election, its first task is electing (or re-electing) a

Speaker (who presides over meetings of the House of Commons) and for MPs to take the oath of allegiance to the Queen. The business of the new Parliament only properly begins the following week when the Queen's Speech, which outlines the new government's legislative programme, is set out in the House of Lords and then debated for four or five days in the House of Commons.

For there to be a Queen's Speech, there needs to be a new government, and the 'principles' of how a new government is formed is also set out in the Cabinet Manual. As it says, the 'ability of a government to command the confidence of the elected House of Commons is central to its authority to govern', although 'confidence' is not the same thing as having a majority or winning every vote; during the 2010-15 Parliament, for example, the Conservative/Liberal Democrat coalition government often lost votes in the House of Commons but remained in office.

When it comes to forming a new government, the incumbent Prime Minister, that is the Prime Minister in office at the point Parliament is dissolved, remains so unless and until he or she resigns. So in 2010, when the incumbent Prime Minister was the Labour leader Gordon Brown, he remained in office despite having 'lost' the election, in that his party had fewer seats than the Conservative Party. But, as the incumbent, he was allowed to attempt to form another government, this time in coalition with the Liberal Democrats and some other smaller parties, although as observers pointed out at the time even had he succeeded Brown would not necessarily have enjoyed a majority in the House of Commons.

9

If such an attempt to form a coalition government fails (as it did in 2010, and also in February 1974 when Tory Edward Heath failed to reach agreement with the Liberals), or if the election result has given one party an overall majority, then the incumbent Prime Minister will resign prior to the Sovereign (the Queen) inviting the person who, as the Cabinet Manual puts it, 'appears most likely to be able to command the confidence of the House to serve as Prime Minister and to form a government'.

Historically, the monarch actually exercised much greater discretion in dismissing Prime Ministers and making a personal choice of successor, but this last occurred in 1834, although 1963 (when Sir Alec Douglas-Home replaced Harold Macmillan as Prime Minister) is often seen as the last occasion on which the Sovereign (then as now Queen Elizabeth) had a degree of choice in deciding who became her Prime Minister. Nowadays, however, convention has it that the monarch should not be drawn into 'party politics', and therefore the onus is firmly upon the political parties represented in Parliament to sort out among themselves who is best placed to become Prime Minister.

There are two possible scenarios following a UK general election:

1 Parliaments with an overall majority in the House of Commons

Following a general election, if the incumbent government maintains an overall majority (as was the case, most recently, in 2001 and 2005), i.e. the number of seats won by the largest party in that election is greater than the combined number of seats for all the other parties in the new Parliament, then it will usually continue in office and carry on with its programme for government. There is no need for the Queen to ask the Prime Minister to continue in office.

If, however, the general election results in an overall majority for a different party (as was the case, most recently, in 1997), then the incumbent Prime Minister and government will immediately resign and the Queen will invite the leader of that party to form a government.

2 Parliaments with no overall majority in the House of Commons

When a general election does not result in an overall majority for any single party then, as outlined above, the incumbent government remains in office unless and until the Prime Minister (and his or her government) submits their resignation to the Queen. An incumbent government, as in 2010, is entitled to wait until the new Parliament has met to explore whether it can command the confidence of the House of Commons, but if this appears unlikely (or there is a clear alternative) it is expected to resign.

Where there is a range of possible administrations (again, as in 2010) then it is likely there will be negotiations between the political parties to establish which combination might be able to command the confidence of the House of Commons and therefore form the next government. The Queen would not be involved in this process, although she would be kept informed of any discussions. In May 2010 the Civil Service provided advice and support to every political party involved in such negotiations, which would probably be the case if this election produces another 'hung' Parliament.

9

In a situation where no single party has an overall majority, there are three possible outcomes:

- Minority government, i.e. the party with (but not always) the largest number of seats opts to govern alone, for example the SNP Scottish Government from 2007 to 2011. The last time this happened in Westminster was in February 1974 when the Labour leader Harold Wilson formed a minority administration, although he did so on the basis that another ballot was due to be held in October 1974. If one party governs as a minority, it could be supported on an issue by issue basis by other parties, as was the case with the SNP in the Scottish Parliament between 2007 and 2011.

- A confidence-and-supply arrangement, in which the party with (but not necessarily) the largest number of MPs decides to govern with informal support from another party, i.e. that smaller party (or parties) will have agreed to vote for its Queen's Speech and support other legislation on a case-by-case basis. Between 1976 and 1977, for example, the Labour government led by James Callaghan agreed a 'pact' (known as The Lib Lab Pact) with David Steel's Liberal Party on this basis (Labour had lost its slim overall majority in the House of Commons as a result of by-election losses and defections).

- A formal coalition government, which is what happened following the 2010 general election, when a government was formed consisting of both Conservative and Liberal Democrat ministers.

9

A coalition of this sort typically commands the confidence of the House of Commons, i.e. it has an overall majority of MPs. Until 2010 the last coalition government in the UK had been during the Second World War.

What will happen following the forthcoming general election is, of course, unpredictable (thus this book), although Jim Murphy, the leader of the Scottish Labour Party, has been keen to emphasise that the 'largest party' in the House of Commons 'forms the next government'. This is both true and false. True for around 80 years because the last time a political party without the largest number of seats formed a government was in the early 1930s, and false in that, as outlined above, what matters constitutionally is the ability to 'command the confidence' of the House of Commons and that, under certain circumstances, could be achieved by a combination of different parties working together, formally or informally.

To 'command the confidence' of the House of Commons, a party or parties needs to reach the magic number of 326 (there are 650 MPs in total). In 2010 David Cameron's Conservative Party won 36.1 per cent of the vote, giving them 306 MPs, while the Labour Party won 29.0 per cent of the vote and secured 258 seats. Because the Conservatives were 20 seats short of an overall majority they negotiated a coalition deal with the Liberal Democrats (which had 57 MPs), therefore taking the two parties to 364, comfortably beyond the 326 threshold.

There is another possible scenario following a general election – although in UK politics it is extremely rare – where one political party can end up with the largest number of votes

9

but not the largest number of MPs, or vice versa. This can occur because the system used to elect the House of Commons is not proportional, or in other words seats are not allocated or 'won' on the basis of each party's share of the vote. There are two examples of this within living memory. In 1951 the Labour Party won a majority of the popular vote but the Conservatives secured more MPs, thus Winston Churchill became Prime Minister, while in February 1974 Edward Heath's Conservative Party won the most votes, but Harold Wilson's Labour Party secured four more MPs, although neither party had an overall majority.

Such a scenario at this election, though not impossible, is unlikely, but here are some more likely outcomes in greater detail:

Majority government
Until the 2010 general election this, whereby either the Conservatives or Labour won an overall majority in the House of Commons, was generally speaking the usual outcome (there were exceptions, for example in February 1974), but this time round most commentators and pollsters are agreed it is extremely unlikely. If it did occur then, as outlined above, either David Cameron would remain Prime Minister but without any Liberal Democrat ministers, or the Labour leader Ed Miliband would form a majority government in his place.

Another Conservative-Liberal Democrat coalition
Although the Liberal Democrats are expected to lose some (if not many) of its MPs at this election, one possible scenario is another coalition between the Conservatives and Liberal Democrats, although there is no guarantee that even the

9

combined strength of the two parties would be enough to secure an overall majority in the House of Commons. Neither has ruled out the prospect, although it should be noted that certain Conservative MPs, including the backbench '1922 Committee' is not keen on the idea of another coalition, while it is possible that the Liberal Democrats – given that its partnership with the Conservatives has arguably lost them support – may decide against another coalition, believing it can best recover while in opposition.

If the Liberal Democrats say no then the Conservatives' coalition options are limited. The SNP and the Greens have unequivocally ruled out helping the Conservatives form another government (formally or informally), while the UK Independence Party has said it would not enter a formal coalition. Nor would Northern Ireland's Democratic Unionist Party (DUP), led by Peter Robinson, which currently has eight MPs in Westminster. It is also possible David Cameron could attempt a minority Tory-Lib Dem coalition, but it would be fragile and unstable even if the numbers added up.

A Labour-Liberal Democrat coalition

If the Labour Party emerges as the largest party after this election, then it is possible it could form a coalition government with the Liberal Democrats. For a long time, at least before the 2010 general election, there was a general expectation that such an arrangement might occur at some stage, although Labour's majorities following the 1997, 2001 and 2005 elections were such that it never had to rely upon a smaller party for support in the House of Commons. Like many political parties, the Liberal Democrats include a broad range of opinions, and many in the party have always been

9

opposed to co-operating with the Conservatives for ideological reasons. If the numbers add up, and it is of course possible they will not, then perhaps the two parties could end up working together.

A confidence-and-supply arrangement

A confidence-and-supply arrangement, under which other parties in the House of Commons informally support a minority administration is another possible scenario, and could apply to either the Conservatives or Labour Party. The lead partner in such a government could be the party which has the largest or second largest number of seats. In that situation – i.e. in another 'hung' Parliament – the Conservatives might negotiate a confidence-and-supply arrangement with, for example, the Liberal Democrats, UKIP and/or the DUP, while Labour might reach such an arrangement with, for example, the Liberal Democrats, Greens and/or SNP. Indeed, the SNP has made it clear this is its preferred option.

The parties signing up would guarantee backing for the government on budgetary matters and confidence issues, but every other vote would be approached on a case-by-case basis. It would be less certain and stable, but would allow smaller parties to feel less bound to the larger parties than in a formal coalition arrangement. A drawback, however, for either David Cameron or Ed Miliband, would be having to tread carefully when it came to certain issues, for example welfare reform and public sector cuts for the Conservatives, or the future of Trident and 'austerity' measures for the Labour Party. Another potential sticking point is the Conservative Party's commitment to holding an in/out referendum on the UK's membership of the European Union by the end of 2017;

9

under a confidence-and-supply this policy might not attract majority support from MPs.

A minority government

Another possible outcome would be if Labour or the Conservatives, assuming either is the largest single party, was to form a minority government, i.e. an administration that did not 'command the confidence' of the House of Commons. As noted above, this last happened in February 1974 when, Edward Heath having failed to reach a deal with the Liberals, Harold Wilson's Labour Party formed a minority government pending another general election.

However, in the devolved Scottish Parliament and National Assembly for Wales there have been more recent examples of minority administrations. Indeed, it has been the case more often than not in the Cardiff Assembly, while in 2007 the SNP formed a highly successful minority government (informally supported by the Scottish Conservatives) which lasted a full Parliamentary term; indeed, the party went on to win an overall majority at the 2011 Holyrood elections.

It is safe to say that a section of the Conservative Party has not enjoyed being in coalition with the Liberal Democrats since 2010 and does not want to repeat the experience after May 2015. Similarly, there are some Labour MPs who believe that if their party wins the largest number of seats then it should govern alone and challenge its opponents to support or vote against its legislative plans. The stakes under such a scenario, however, would be high: there would be no guarantee that a minority Conservative or Labour government would win enough support for its major Bills, or indeed survive a full Parliamentary term.

A 'rainbow' coalition

A 'rainbow' coalition is thus named because it includes a number of different parties which all use different colours. In 2010 the SNP's Angus Robertson suggested that Labour, the Liberal Democrats, Plaid Cymru and the SNP join forces to form a red/orange/green/yellow rainbow coalition, while this time round SNP Nicola Sturgeon has proposed a 'progressive alliance' of the SNP, Plaid and Greens, which might also form part of a rainbow coalition with the Labour Party. There is no precedent for this, however, in UK politics.

A 'grand' coalition

In some European countries, for example Germany, a 'grand' coalition is the term given to an alliance of the two biggest parties in Parliament. This has only happened at Westminster in exceptional circumstances, for example during wartime or as a result of the 'Depression' in the 1930s. Few observers believe it is likely as a result of the 2015 general election, although speaking in a House of Lords debate on the NHS, the Conservative peer Lord Cormack suggested a grand coalition of Labour and the Conservatives might be 'an infinitely preferable solution to the SNP holding the balance of power'. Similarly, the former Labour Cabinet minister Charles Clarke said that outcome should not be 'unthinkable'.

For more information about these outcomes, please see www.gov.uk/government/uploads/system/uploads/attachment_data/file/60641/cabinet-manual.pdf

Constitutional Implications

In Scotland, the forthcoming general election takes place in the long shadow of last year's independence referendum. The political parties involved are, of course, the same, as are many of the main campaigners and, indeed, the arguments: austerity, Europe, more devolution for Scotland, the price of oil, and so on.

Until the year 2000 the SNP argued that if it won a majority of Scottish seats at a Westminster election then that would represent a 'mandate' to begin independence negotiations, but that is no longer the case. For the past 15 years Nationalists have made it clear that independence can only happen following a referendum, and for a referendum to happen (as in 2011–14) the SNP would need a majority of MSPs in the devolved Scottish Parliament.

First Minister Nicola Sturgeon has yet to decide whether her party's manifesto for next year's Holyrood elections will include a commitment to hold another referendum (her predecessor as First Minister, Alex Salmond, had previously said that the September 2014 Referedum would be a 'once-in-a-generation' event), so in that context even if the SNP won every Scottish constituency on 7 May it would not in itself bring independence any closer to becoming reality.

The outcome of the 2015 general election, however, could have constitutional implications for Scotland as well as the rest of the United Kingdom.

Extra powers for the Scottish Parliament

The three main Unionist parties – the Conservatives, Labour and the Liberal Democrats – all committed before the general election to implement 'draft clauses' based on the recommendations of the cross-party Smith Commission convened after the independence referendum. This including, among other powers, the full devolution of income tax and control over Air Passenger Duty to the Scottish Parliament, as well as responsibility for future Scottish Parliament elections elections and greater discretion over welfare payments. Because of this commitment, and the fact that some combination of those parties is likely to form the next government, a new Scotland Bill is likely to feature in the next Queen's Speech in May or June 2015.

The SNP, which also took part in the Smith Commission, has argued that the 'draft clauses' published by the previous UK government in January 2015 'watered down' some of Lord Smith's recommendations, and thus it has promised that if it ends up supporting the Labour Party under a confidence-and-supply arrangement after the forthcoming election then it will ensure that the recommendations are implemented in full. Furthermore, the SNP also says its goal after this election is to achieve 'devo-max' for Scotland, i.e. devolution of all powers except defence and foreign affairs.

A constitutional convention

For the last few years there have been growing calls from some Unionists for a UK-wide constitutional convention, perhaps modelled on the cross-party Scottish Constitutional Convention which helped design the blueprint for a devolved Scottish Parliament in the late 1980s and early 1990s. This was cross-party (although the Conservatives and SNP were not involved) but also included representatives from 'civic Scotland', trade unionists, faith groups, and so on.

Some proponents of a UK convention argue that it should be constituted in a similar way, with the broader goal of drawing together different constitutional debates in Scotland, England, Wales and Northern Ireland and coming up with a more holistic approach to reform. Many, including the Liberal Democrats, view such a convention as the first step towards creating a genuinely 'federal' UK with a written constitution, an elected Senate and regional assemblies in England.

Interestingly William Hague, who until the election was Leader of the House of Commons, did not rule out a constitutional convention but argued that it could not include already existing discussions, for example English Votes for English Laws.

English Votes for English Laws

English Votes for English Laws (known as 'EVEL' in some quarters) is an idea that has been floating around since the creation of a devolved Scottish Parliament in 1999. Devolution in Scotland and Wales gave rise to what the former Ulster Unionist MP Enoch Powell dubbed the 'West Lothian Question'. This was a reference to the former Labour MP Tam Dalyell (who represented West Lothian in the House of Commons), who first pointed out the discrepancy by which, under devolution, a Westminster MP for West Lothian could vote on matters affecting the English town of Blackburn in Lancashire but not on matters concerning Blackburn in his or her own constituency, because certain powers would have been devolved to Edinburgh.

The former Labour Lord Chancellor Derry Irvine once joked that the best way to deal with the West Lothian Question was 'not to ask it', but in more than 15 years of devolution its

10

salience among English MPs and voters has steadily increased, with critics pointing to a few occasions on which support from Scottish MPs resulted in England-only measures like top-up tuition fees and foundation hospitals becoming law. Although such cases are rare in the House of Commons, many believe it is a constitutional anomaly that requires correction.

The Commission on the consequences of devolution for the House of Commons, also known as the McKay Commission, reported in March 2013 and recommended that future legislation affecting England but not other parts of the UK should require the support of a majority of MPs sitting for English constituencies. In February 2015, meanwhile, William Hague set out a slightly different conclusion, that:

- **English MPs would be given a veto over legislation that applies only in England, including setting income tax rates (because income tax are being devolved fully to Holyrood under the Smith Commission's recommendations).**

- **MPs from other parts of the UK, outside of England, would still be able to debate laws that apply solely in England, as a Commons majority would still be required for any bill to pass.**

- **The committee stage of putting a bill together, when detailed line-by-line scrutiny takes place, would be restricted solely to those MPs who represent English constituencies.**

If the Conservatives form a majority government after this election, then they say they will introduce legislation to make these proposals law. Labour and the Liberal Democrats, however, are not enthusiastic about this, while the SNP (which previously supported EVEL on an informal basis) now says it will vote on England-only matters if there is a clear knock-on impact in Scotland, for example when it comes to Barnett 'consequentials', i.e. public spending cuts (or increases) as a result to changes in government funding for health and education south of the border. Other critics say EVEL would create 'two classes of MPs' and thus diminish the standing of Scottish MPs in the House of Commons.

Electoral reform

One consequence of the 2010 coalition agreement between the Conservatives and Liberal Democrats was a UK-wide referendum (only the second since the 1975 European plebiscite) on electoral reform, specifically the introduction of the 'Alternative Vote' (AV) for elections to the House of Commons. Held on the same day as the 2011 Holyrood elections, the result was decisive: 68 per cent of voters wanted to retain first-past-the-post, while 32 per cent voted for AV.

By common consent the outcome of this referendum set back the campaign for electoral reform quite significantly, although supporters of other proportional representation systems argue that AV was not an attractive option and therefore failed to garner support. After all, devolved assemblies and parliaments based in London, Cardiff, Belfast and Edinburgh are all elected by PR, as are the UK's representatives in the European Parliament, not to forget local government in Scotland and Northern Ireland.

Traditionally, the main argument for first-past-the-post was that it produces governments with strong majorities. That, of

10

course, was not the case in 2010 and nor does it look likely to be the case again in 2015. It is possible, therefore, that the campaign for electoral reform may get a boost from another 'hung' Parliament. If, for example, the last general election had been fought under a PR system then the Labour Party would have won 25 seats in Scotland, the SNP 12, the Liberal Democrats 11 (actually the number that party secured in 2010) and the Conservatives 10 (instead of just one).

An in/out referendum on the UK and EU

In January 2013 Prime Minister David Cameron promised an 'in/out' referendum on the UK's membership of the European Union by the end of 2017, following a period of renegotiation with the EU. This, however, will only happen if the Conservative Party wins an outright majority at this general election. Both Labour and the Liberal Democrats oppose the policy of guaranteeing a referendum in 2017, instead arguing that one should only be held if there is a further transfer of sovereignty to the EU, i.e. following another Treaty revision.

Since 2010, polls have shown that the UK electorate is divided on the question, with opposition peaking in November 2012 at 56 per cent compared to 30 per cent who wanted to remain and support peaking in 2013. Surveys also indicate that there are statistically significant (though not huge) differences in public opinion in Wales and Scotland, where voters tend to be more pro-European, or probably more accurately less Euro-sceptic than those in England. In late 2014, meanwhile, SNP leader Nicola Sturgeon argued that in order for a vote favouring withdrawal from the EU to take effect (although she opposes a referendum being held at all) then every part of the

UK would have to endorse that aim, a so-called quadruple lock. Polls suggest that around a third of Scots favour withdrawal from the EU.

Another general election?

There is one other constitutional scenario, and that is the prospect of another general election being held before 2020 when, under the Fixed-term Parliaments Act, it is scheduled to take place. An early election would take place, according the 'Cabinet Manual', in two circumstances:

- **The first is where two-thirds of the membership of the House of Commons agree that it is right that there should be a general election immediately and pass a motion 'that there shall be an early Parliamentary general election'.**

- **The other circumstance is where a government has lost a motion that 'this House has no confidence in Her Majesty's Government' and no government has, within a 14-day period, secured a motion that 'this House has confidence in Her Majesty's Government'. In either of these cases, the date of the election is set by the Sovereign by Proclamation on the advice of the Prime Minister and dissolution occurs 17 working days before the date appointed for the election.**

The Fixed-term Parliaments Act, however, does not have many fans within the Conservative and Labour Parties and it is possible that it may be repealed shortly after the 2015 general election.

10

Policy Grid

	Conservatives	Greens	Labour	Liberal Democrats	SNP	UKIP
RESERVED						
Economy	Plans to eradicate the current deficit 'as soon as possible' in the next Parliament.	Committed to an economic policy not solely driven by growth, but by 'quality of life'. Promises to end austerity and restore the public sector. Committed to the Living Wage and a Citizens Income.	Ed Miliband has said there 'is no path to growth and prosperity for working people which does not tackle the deficit', but Labour would do so more gradually than the Conservatives.	Like the Conservatives, the Liberal Democrats have committed to eliminating the budget deficit by 2018–19, but unlike the Conservatives they will do so partly through tax rises (see below).	Promises an 'alternative to austerity' by limiting growth in departmental spending to 0.5 per cent each year, meaning £180 billion more in public spending in the next Parliament (across the UK). Committed to 'fairer increases in the minimum wage'.	Pledges to repair the economy by leaving the EU and saving £8 billion per year and by cutting foreign aid budget by £9 billion per year, scrapping green subsidies and abolishing the Department for Culture Media and Sport.
Taxation	Reduce income tax (by increasing the personal tax allowance) for 25 million people. Will freeze fuel duty and also increase inheritance tax threshold.	New wealth tax on the top 1 per cent, a 'Robin Hood Tax' on the banks and the closure of tax loopholes.	Committed to reducing taxes for those on low and middle incomes, but also plan to restore the 10p and 50p tax rates, introduce a 'Mansion Tax' and a bankers' bonus.	Plans to increase the personal tax allowance to £12,500, but would also raise £8 billion from higher earners, for example by 'aligning' Capital Gains Tax more closely with income tax.	Will consider restoring the 50p income tax rate, but does not propose a bankers' or Mansion tax.	Pledges to increase personal allowance to £13,500, abolish inheritance tax, and introduce a 35p income tax rate for those earning between £42,285 and £55,000.
Welfare	Pledges to freeze working-age benefits for two years from April 2015, to lower the benefits cap from £26,000 to £23,000 and to oblige young people unemployed for six months to be in training or to work for their benefits.	Committed to rolling back welfare cuts and Universal Credit, and abolishing Bedroom Tax and Workfare.	Committed to scrapping the Bedroom Tax and will also 'pause' rollout of the current government's Universal Credit scheme if it wins in 2015.	Would raise benefits – but excluding pensions and disability payments – by 1 per cent a year.	Argues that responsibility for all benefits should be devolved. Committed to halting Personal Independence Payments and Universal Credit in Scotland. Opposed to Bedroom Tax. Committed to protecting Basic State Pension.	Supports a streamlined welfare system and benefit cap. Opposed to Bedroom Tax. Child benefit to be restricted to permanent residents of the UK, and limited to first two children.

	Conservatives	Greens	Labour	Liberal Democrats	SNP	UKIP
RESERVED						
Foreign Affairs	Committed to standing up for 'British values' and defending borders with 'an immigration system that puts British people first'.	Recognises that co-operation is needed at 'a global level' in order to secure 'sustainable societies' in the UK.	Labour will conduct a 'wide-ranging review' of the UK's international and diplomatic priorities. It would also 'reform and repair' Britain's relationship with the EU while placing a 'renewed focus' on relations with Asia.	Say they are the only party that 'truly understands' that the UK is 'stronger in the world' when it works with other countries and remains a 'strong player' in Europe. Wants to increase trade to China, India and Brazil.	Wants an 'ethical' foreign policy and is opposed to 'illegal' wars and occupation.	Would target foreign aid at healthcare initiatives with a 'much-reduced' aid budget.
Europe	Promises an 'in/out' referendum on the UK's membership of the EU by the end of 2017.	Supports EU membership but opposes the EU's 'market-obsessed' economic model.	Would only support an EU referendum if and when there is a transfer of more powers to Brussels.	Would only support an EU referendum if and when there is a transfer of more powers to Brussels.	Committed to Scotland remaining part of the EU. Opposes an in/out referendum but wants a 'quadruple lock' if it goes ahead.	Committed to withdrawing UK from membership of the EU.
Defence	In late 2014, Defence Secretary Michael Fallon pledged that there would be £3.3 billion of new investment in naval bases, securing 7,500 jobs in Portsmouth, Devonport and on the Clyde.	Supports reforming the UN Security Council to reduce influence of arms dealers and ensure fair representation.	Says it has 'learnt the lessons of the past' in rushing to military action and intervention abroad. Need a 'wide-ranging' and 'open' debate about future of UK defence policy.	Its 2013 party conference adopted a policy proposing to 'reassess the UK's place in the world and the military capabilities to enable us to achieve it'.	In an independent Scotland the SNP would set up a Scottish Defence Force, armed forces with an air base, a non-nuclear naval base and a mobile armed brigade.	Pledges that the UK should resource fully its military assets and personnel. Will guarantee those who have served in the armed force a minimum of 12 years' work in the police force, prison service or border force.
Trident	Would proceed with Trident replacement.	Will actively campaign against Trident renewal.	Would proceed with Trident replacement but open to the idea of one less submarine.	Wants to reduce the number of Trident submarines, 'saving costs' and making the UK's nuclear defence system 'fit for the 21st century'.	Opposed to the renewal of Trident and, if retained, wants it relocated outside Scottish territory.	Committed to maintaining Trident, but considering reducing number of submarines.

	Conservatives	Greens	Labour	Liberal Democrats	SNP	UKIP
RESERVED						
Constitutional	Proposes to legislate for 'EVEL', or English Votes for English Laws, and will introduce a new Scotland Bill. Open to the idea of a UK-wide constitutional convention.	The Scottish Green Party supports independence for Scotland and will continue to do so.	Proposes a UK-wide constitutional convention to be formed in late 2015. Supports regional devolution in England and a new Scotland Bill.	Wants 'Home Rule' for Scotland as part of a 'federal' United Kingdom. Also supports electoral reform and a new Scotland Bill.	Will pressure the three main UK parties to implement the Smith Commission recommendations in full.	Supports English Votes for English Laws, Swiss-style 'direct democracy' and the creation of a federal UK.
TTIP (Transatlantic Trade and Investment Partnership)	Supporting TTIP is part of the Conservatives' 'long-term economic plan' to increase growth and promote trade.	Opposed to TTIP, says it is a 'corporate power grab' that 'must be stopped'.	Supports TTIP but wants the NHS to be 'excluded' from its scope.	Supports the inclusion of safeguards in TTIP and other trade agreements to allow governments to regulate health and environmental protection.	Supports a 'veto' of TTIP unless the NHS is 'fully and clearly exempted' from the agreement.	Supports TTIP.
Fracking	David Cameron has said that fracking has 'real potential to drive energy bills down'.	Supports a moratorium on fracking.	Says shale gas extraction must only be permitted with 'robust regulation' and 'comprehensive monitoring'.	In 2013 Nick Clegg gave 'cautious' support to fracking, although a lot of Liberal Democrats are opposed.	Supports a moratorium on fracking.	Supports fracking.
Immigration	Supports reduced access to benefits for immigrants. Would discourage illegal immigration by restricting access to work, housing and healthcare. Introduce new citizen test emphasising 'British values'.	Would abandon an 'artificial immigration cap' and ensure a healthy labour market.	No benefits for immigrants for at least two years after entering the country. Aims to control immigration with stronger border controls, and a new law to prevent employers exploiting immigrants with unfair wages.	Says 'more control' is needed to 'stop people breaking the rules'. Would introduce 'exit checks' so government can keep track of who is leaving the country and overstaying visas.	Wants immigration policy to be devolved. Committed to reintroducing the post-study work visa, lowering financial maintenance thresholds and minimum salary levels for entry.	Recognises benefits of limited, controlled immigration: 'Those coming to work in the UK must have a job to go to, must speak English, must have accommodation agreed prior to their arrival'.

	Conservatives	Greens	Labour	Liberal Democrats	SNP	UKIP
CURRENTLY DEVOLVED						
Education	Pursue a reform agenda on education based on school diversity, school autonomy and parental choice.	Move educational policy away from simply making people work-ready towards encouraging creativity and accessibility.	Guarantee an apprenticeship for every school leaver with basic grades. Smaller class sizes for five, six and seven-year-olds.	Guarantees education funding from nursery to college.	Promises to maintain a policy of free tuition at Scottish universities.	Pledges to introduce option for school students to take an apprenticeship qualification instead of secondary school qualifications.
Housing	Pledges to deliver 100,000 new homes for first-time buyers, make 10,000 new affordable homes available at below market rent and extend the Equity Loan part of Help to Buy to 2020. Proposes Right to Buy for Housing Association tenants.	Encourages community ownership of houses through co-operatives and housing associations.	Supports building 200,000 homes a year by 2020. Support renters by introducing longer-term tenancies and banning inflated letting fees.	In 2014 Nick Clegg said the Conservatives' failure to invest in housing was 'unfair and economically unsustainable'. Promise to 'control' another housing boom.	Opposes the 'right to buy' (which the SNP has abolished in Scotland) and will continue to prioritise affordable housing.	Pledges to protect the Green Belt, and make it easier to build on brownfield instead of greenfield sites.
Justice	Wants Scottish Government to conduct a review of Police Scotland to address issues of 'accountability'.	Aims to reduce crime and prison populations by moving to community-based sentences and reparation.	Would look at extending the youth justice system to the age of 21.	Would divert people with drug and mental health problems away from the criminal justice system and reduce the number of women in prison.	Says Scotland is 'safer today than it was four years ago' and it is 'working hard to make it even safer'.	Will withdraw from the jurisdiction of the European Court of Human Rights. Opposes votes for prisoners.

	Conservatives	Greens	Labour	Liberal Democrats	SNP	UKIP
CURRENTLY DEVOLVED						
Enterprise	Would support small business and enterprise with infrastructure and lower jobs taxes.	Promises to invest millions in sustainable jobs and enterprise.	Says it would 'recognise and support' enterprise in order to 'modernise and reform' the UK's economy.	Will continue to encourage local authorities, Local Enterprise Partnerships and City Deals to work with investors and local businesses.	Has a vision of Scotland having an economy that 'increasingly benefits from high-paid and high-quality jobs in the emerging industries like life-sciences, renewable energy and the creative sector'.	Would allow businesses to discriminate in favour of young British workers.
NHS	Wants Scottish Government to reintroduce prescription charges to raise funds for 1,000 more nurses.	Committed to halting the 'privatisation' of the NHS.	Committed to 'securing the future of the NHS' with 20,000 more nurses and 8,000 more GPs.	Pledges to meet the funding shortfall of £8 billion in the NHS by 2020. Would also invest £500 million each year in mental health.	Would support 'restoring' the NHS in England while 'protecting' Scotland's NHS budget.	Committed to ensuring the NHS is free at point of delivery for all UK residents. Immigrants would require private health insurance as a condition of entry.

The positions of each of the parties on the above reserved and devolved policy issues have been summarised from publicly available information. There may be variations once each party has published its election manifesto. Voters are encouraged to seek clarification from their local parliamentary candidates at hustings or by contacting them direct. Details of candidates are available from your local elections office, see www.aboutmyvote.co.uk.

Timeline

2015

30 March	Dissolution of Parliament.
20 April	Voter registration deadline.
21 April	Deadline for applications for postal vote.
28 April	Deadline for applications for proxy vote.
7 May	General Election 2015. Polling booths open 7am – 10pm. Counting of votes commences at 10pm.
8 May	Count continues. Parties likely to consider possible formal coalitions or informal arrangements in the event of a hung parliament.
c. 8 May	New government is formed.
c. 19 May	New Parliament meets to swear in MPs and elect a Speaker.
c. 26 May	Queen's Speech (important test of new government's support, will also include a new Scotland Bill to give legislative effect to Smith Commission recommendations). Budget statement (only if there's a change of government) If the government loses the 'confidence' of the House of Commons then there is a 14-day period in which another administration can be formed. Failing that, another election will be held on a date set by 'proclamation' and Parliament dissolved 17 days before that date.

Finance Bill introduced to Parliament (either giving effect to George Osborne's March 2015 statement or the new government's post-election Budget)

Introduction of legislation to give effect to English Votes for English Laws (only if election produces a Conservative or possibly a Conservative-led government).

2016

April   Major aspects of 2012 Scotland Act take effect (i.e. the creation of a new 'Scottish' rate of income tax).

5 May   Scottish Parliament elections

2017

By 31 December   Referendum to decide whether UK should remain part of the EU, only in the event of a Conservative majority (or possibly if there is a Conservative-led coalition after May 2015 election).

Luath Press Limited

committed to publishing well written books worth reading

LUATH PRESS takes its name from Robert Burns, whose little collie Luath (*Gael.*, swift or nimble) tripped up Jean Armour at a wedding and gave him the chance to speak to the woman who was to be his wife and the abiding love of his life. Burns called one of 'The Twa Dogs' Luath after Cuchullin's hunting dog in Ossian's *Fingal*. Luath Press was established in 1981 in the heart of Burns country, and now resides a few steps up the road from Burns' first lodgings on Edinburgh's Royal Mile.

Luath offers you distinctive writing with a hint of unexpected pleasures.

Most bookshops in the UK, the US, Canada, Australia, New Zealand and parts of Europe either carry our books in stock or can order them for you. To order direct from us, please send a £sterling cheque, postal order, international money order or your credit card details (number, address of cardholder and expiry date) to us at the address below. Please add post and packing as follows: UK – £1.00 per delivery address; overseas surface mail – £2.50 per delivery address; overseas airmail – £3.50 for the first book to each delivery address, plus £1.00 for each additional book by airmail to the same address. If your order is a gift, we will happily enclose your card or message at no extra charge.

Luath Press Limited
543/2 Castlehill
The Royal Mile
Edinburgh EH1 2ND
Scotland
Telephone: 0131 225 4326 (24 hours)
Fax: 0131 225 4324
email: sales@luath.co.uk
Website: www.luath.co.uk